Dhvani and Structuralist Poetics

Multicultural Studies of
Creation of Meaning in Poetry

For My Father

Late Professor Harinathendra Guru

Dhvani and Structuralist Poetics

Multicultural Studies of Creation of Meaning in Poetry

Bhavatosh Indraguru
Vikalp Parashar

DK PRINTWORLD
Publishers of Indian Traditions

Cataloging in Publication Data – DK
[Courtesy: D.K. Printworld (P) Ltd. indology@dkprintworld.com]

Indraguru, Bhavatosh, 1968-
Dhvani and structuralist poetics : multicultural studies of creation of meaning in poetry / Bhavatosh Indraguru, Vikalp Parashar.
p. cm.
Includes bibliographical references (p.).
ISBN 13: 9788124606346

1. Dhvani (Poetics) 2. Poetics. 3. Sanskrit poetry — History and criticism. I. Parashar, Vikalp, 1983-, joint author. II. Title.

DDC 891.2109 23

First published in India, 2012
ISBN 13: 978-81-246-0634-6 **ISBN 10: 81-246-0634-X**

Published and printed by:
D.K. Printworld (P) Ltd.
Regd. Office : *'Vedaśrī'*, F-395, Sudarshan Park
(Metro Station: Ramesh Nagar), New Delhi - 110 015
Phones : (011) 2545 3975; 2546 6019; *Fax* : (011) 2546 5926
E-mail : indology@dkprintworld.com
Web : www.dkprintworld.com

Preface

AN ideal event of artistic creation manifests and presupposes the necessity of continuity, progression, generation and finally the modification from an occasional and particular notation to a significant suggestion inasmuch as the categories that participate in its enrichment, expansion, signification and universalisation themselves undergo a radical change in both, the form and content. To that extent, artistry intentionally projects itself through the grounds of synthesis and transformation. It must be added that every category of expression (for example, *śabda, pada, varṇa, vākya, bhāva, vibhāva, anubhāva, sthāyībhāva, sañcārībhāva, ālambana, uddīpana*) composes itself around the multiplicity of variables, which are either converging on or are synchronised along a fixed coordinate. This is essentially the groundwork for the commencement of a lengthened and necessarily dignified precedure of change where the purport is to bring about the equivalents in concrete universals. The argumentative concern underlying the situation, out of necessity, has attracted the attention of theoreticians both in Indian and the Western intellectual traditions. Accordingly, *dhvani* (Indian critical system developed around the eighth century CE) and the Structuralist poetics (Western critical premise commencing with Ferdinand de Saussure's Course in General Linguistics) substantiate an adequate methodology to understand the formation of categories, contents, constructs and mediums as a necessary corollary to an analytical precedure that would bring about transformation, and, would consequently end up with the emergence of a qua work of art. Ānandavardhana, the progenitor of *dhvani* system, suggests the independent universalisation of *śabda, pada, varṇa, vākya, bhāva, vibhāva, anubhāva, sthāyībhāva, sañchārībhāva, ālambana, uddīpana* for the sake of an absolute artistic formation. Similarly, the Structuralist poetics (following Saussure, Barthes, Jakobson and others) focuses on the need and necessity to explicate words, letters, syllables and even otherwise an experience, so as to completely create a valid notation out of each of these for the sake of totality in the meaning formation. This is essentially the reality of contention that would propose a sequence of identities and an assertion thus bringing about the truth of exposition.

The worth and intention of a study of this nature are primarily born out of the fact that Indian and the Western scholarships have not paid much of attention on this subject. The significance thereof, therefore, is immediate, forthwith and a brilliant one in that it promotes the proper understanding and facilitates the enjoyment of literature. Should it be brought to the construction of the categories of appreciation, the effort will have its meaning and significance! In preparation of a work of this demanding nature, the scholarship has been immensely strengthened by the constant criticism brought about by my wife Nisha. I, therefore, put my sincere thanks for her on the record.

Bhavatosh Indraguru

Contents

Introduction

I

THE comprehension of an artistic situation manifests varieties of composite units and parts through which the possibility of reinventing further refined models and absolute categories could be successfully worked out. And, it is also remarkable to understand that the event of assertion made by the comprehensibility, in fact, attends to the aspect of resolution, transformation, modification, generation and transmutation of an object into an event. It is, in this context, that the strength of an artistic situation could be rightly examined and explained through perceptible categories of appreciation and the preoccupation of theoretical method would necessarily enlarge the range and extent of idealistic configuration. This situation is basic to the canonical framework developed for the purpose in Indian and the European methods of obtaining equivalents for inquisition, enquiry, explication and the like. For that matter, *dhvani* and structuralist poetics emerge as the two primary theoretical frameworks in which the reality of inquisition and propagation of comprehensibility and creativity of the artistry could be so well conceived, exposed and implied. In each of these systems, the maturity of conception and universality of expression of the content, context and the medium are quite remarkable; thus the exposition of creative content for the sake of an equally idealised artistry becomes a notional and conceptual framework. It is, however, to be admitted that the Indian situation tends to lay more emphasis on the cognitive and speculative urgency so as to build up large-scale models of universality in an artistry. While the Western structuralist poetics conforms to an admittance of the principle of immediacy in the resolution of object and event, yet, however, the standard of categorisation and intention of appreciation, in relation to an absolute and supra-rational form of an artistic situation, upholds the worth of a common pursuit of excellence. To this end, the inculcation of terms of comparison and subsequent explication could hold up to the variety and precision affecting a credit of perception under the circumstances of perceptability of having an excess through the implicated and implied categories, the expansion of evaluative measures, would, therefore be worthy of attention.

II

In *dhvani* system, the aspect of absolute artistry intending an ideal and significant perspective, includes purity, refinement, elegance, precision in the manners in which the linguistic and emotive categories are composed, conceived and constituted. The effect of precision is felt squarely in equal concretisation of contents, constructs and models which participate under the exceptional principality of a well-designated and approved form. Ānandavardhana, in the eighth century CE, had displayed the wisdom and brilliance in elevating the substance of such a contention to the extreme, and, at the same time, developed the theoretical form, understood and explained as *dhvani*. This theory, while holding the highest standards in terms of organisation and application of the category, carefully develops the principles of artistic creation. Accordingly, in order to create an ideal artistry, in keeping with the principle of Ānandavardhana, there shall have to be a conscious and inductive necessity to propagate a reasonable understanding of almost every content, every construct, every model, every context and every medium. For this reason, an artistry could be seen, realised, understood and visualised, as if it is prone to the utmost division so that one could understand the significance of every unit and every part, and subsequently every division manifest in the isolation and bifurcation of every unit and part, would find a proper assortment by the way of converging themselves into the significant act of idealisation. It is, thus, division of an existing category and evolution of a new category in terms of the coherence of an intended and absolute, which becomes the fundamental necessity, in accordance with the laws of creativity developed by Ānandavardhana. Inasmuch as the presupposition of what is intended as an ideal, must begin with the division of a form into content and must end by completing the process of evolution, it would be, of necessity, the requirement that linguistic and emotive categories are first isolated and then brought to the condition of rationalisation. In this regard, the linguistic categories are brought forth through the correlation of properties inherent in *śabda* (word) as one of the important segments of creation of an art. *Śabda,* as a category, is effective in initiating the versions of associative forms, which themselves acquire the shape of dependent categorical situation. Thus, the complete linguistic system would be one in which there would be the intensity of modification suggested by the artistic turn that each receives and begets as the creativity advances. Subsequently, we can understand that *śabda, pada* (group of words), *varṇa* (syllable), *vākya* (sentence) are the primary locations where the maturity of content in terms of the growth of the linguistic foundations could be successfully observed. Ānandavardhana has a point in stating the fact that the identification of the contents in the categories; categories in the content; models in the categories and categories in the models, are the preliminary groundworks which are to be convincingly brought about. At the beginning, the process of formulation is based on what one could find as an extensive network of relations and interrelations within each concrete term. Therefore, *śabda* is indispensable by the virtue of segmental completion that it could bring about. On the other hand, initiation of *śabda* as the point of advancing assertion may invite a range of phonetic, syntactic, morphological and semiotic figures which are both historically, culturally and artistically expressive. It would mean, in the second place, that *śabda* is displaced and moved and thus the entire system is figuratively and contentively implied in being supplemented by the greatest range of approved figures and functions, so necessary to build up strength in the artistic form. The manner is based on the needs and necessities of both, the context and the medium, and thus *śabda* as the factor of production of phonological universals would also be, at the same time, exactly a deducible relation to effect large-scale changes in the other structures which are similarly produced for the sake of building up factor and variables in the artistry. Besides *śabda*, it could also be demonstrated that the cumulation is strongly felt in the relative situation where *varṇa, pada* and *vākya* come together and give rise to a direct distortion of the fact contained in the advancement of the situation. The figure that is most suited for the purpose of approving an absolute form and concrete term is an organised whole that emerges out of the process of inter-transmutation and, on that account, the need of division becomes justifiable, progressing and expanding *śabda, pada, varṇa* and *vākya* shall have an exact statement of denotation only by virtue of the consideration that each one is dispersed to the greatest possible limit. In the process of dispersion, there is also the maximum probability of selection of the right content and it is accomplished exactly at this stage. While the linguistic contents approach optimum concretisation, there is also the significant revelation of an equivalent form in terms of categorical conjunction, and because of this, we have the experiential side that is as important as the linguistic form. Ānandavardhana goes on to suggest that every intensity of perception generated in language, is simultaneously suited to similar event of actual form in the conduct of experience as a factor of artistic production. Experience involves the constitution of categories like *bhāva, vibhāva, sthāyībhāva, anubhāva, sañcārībhāva, ālambana, uddīpana* in such a way that each of these is capable of establishing a foundation of standard aesthetic configuration. To begin with, *bhāva* is the principal factor in which every concrete figure is originated and it stabilises both, the sensation and intellection. The concordance between sensation and intellection, so as to institute the condition of transformation of every sensory and intellectional category within the complete form, is one of the significant functions to be observed in this connection. In *bhāva,* what is initiated is the manner of prospective structure that the other categories (*sthāyībhāva* and the like) would acquire, and following this at every major event of coordination, the content is made to modify itself into the medium in that the two similar constructs would be brought together so as to compare the structural and functional equivalences. The progression of *bhāva* in such a manner leads to the building up of universals at several junctions, and, while artistry is at the end of every universal accord itself to a definite semantic projection. The contents that originate in *bhāva,* as a part of universality and significance, are further strengthened by another important category in *sthāyībhāva* through which primordial separation of form and content, context and medium and context and context is realistically fixed up and exposed to determinate meaning forms. It is, therefore, an act to synthesise any disintegration whatsoever, that might be forthcoming in the artistic situation. For that matter, *sthāyībhāva*s explain the emergence of nine idealistic expressions of determinate significance as long as the consideration is made for the sake of artistic existence. These nine forms are the exceptional modes of synthesis which govern the cultural, religious, historical and social universalisation of the collective human perception. The eventuality of prospective absolute that inheres upon stylistic or formalistic regeneration of a conceptual form, is one of the major methods of conceptual recognisation brought about by the *sthāyībhāva*s. The term of this effect is prolonged and stabilised till an exact and conditionally operative form is having its emergence, and, from this standpoint, the manner of application conceived in *sthāyībhāva*s is essentially one that correlates the point of origin and the point of end. In artistic consideration, the *sthāyībhāva*s are approved in accordance with the attitude, the method, the commitment and even the level of conviction associated with the process of idealisation continuously and throughout the artistry. It is, for that matter, an issue of debate. The applicability of *sthāyībhāva*s could be understood to be applicable just at the point of significance having the greatest intensity of experience or language models. In each of the situations, the extent of modification and the length of resolution stand in effective harmony with each other, and thus, there can be an immediate approval of the functional method. Similarly, the product that comes out of secondary organisation suggested in *sthāyībhāva*, is opened for communication and transference at two stages which are themselves induced by other categorical apparatuses known as *vibhāva* and *anubhāva*. The *vibhāva*s enhance and accelerate the collection of events, objects, subjects and the form purported to define an experiential situation and, for this reason, when experience is brought to recognition of the artist, it is forthwith routed through exact terms and figures, and, in turn, each of these becomes the agencies of communication in that each receives and refracts the experience to the next order of inception. It is now significantly reasonable choice presented by the *vibhāva*s for the sake of the conduction of an artistic situation. It, thus, states the fact that hetrogeneity of artistry, by the act of transference of exact poetic material through concrete object/event, is turned into a homogeneous order of conception. *Vibhāva*s are generally rich in performing an approved version of synthetical function in which the consolidation of unitary artistic effect, at least at the level of presentation and exposition, seems to be worthy of consideration. The chronology and the sequence of the carrier of experience are so thoroughgoing that every conceivable content of experience is recreated into its significant variants. The next category, that does the work of reception of the externally organised experiential forms, is *anubhāva*. *Anubhāva*s are those primordial forms which enact and orient the experiential contents towards more organisation, by codifying the whole into the finally built-up sequence of transmutation and in the final analysis each of the external experiential content is transmogrified, thus bringing about the final version of artistic form and situation. The role played by *anubhāva*s is to be understood in terms of the enhancement of the rate of creativity, and thus, also for the sake of unifying the crudeness of external observation and reasonable meaningfulness of the internal artistic form. In other words, we can say that *anubhāva*s are precisely the factors which determine and fix up the semantic absolute for the sake of comprehensibility by the readers or even by the general audience who would invariably be the agents of reception. The formation of circumstances, for the sake of an experience, is conditionally and functionally operative in consequence of the richness brought forth at the behest of *ālambana* (stimulus) and *uddīpana* (stimulant). The manner of progression of the events would be assuredly underlying in the revival of committed position from where the aspects of universality are decided. In this segment, the last reasonable category that brings about the concentration, equilibrium, poise and balance, is the *sañcārībhāva*s. *Sañcārībhāva*s are to be defined in terms of the distribution of contents along the equal distance, therefore, in these instruments, there is nothing that could be held out to be fixed, certain or permanent. This is a term of change in the constitution and property depending on the nature of content and the medium. As a part of shifting sensory impressions, *sañcārībhāvas* induct the enriched content, both by the homogeneous and heterogeneous modes. In the homogeneous modes, they bring about the perfection of emotive models and thus project the fact of synthesis as one of the necessary and reliable circumstances. In a heterogeneous situation, on the other hand, the event of correlation is aggravated to such a great extent that language forms the experiential varieties that are brought to stay as the two corresponding situations. In this way, the artistry progresses and acquires structurally competent models for perpetuation and prolongation. With these categories as the necessary events in the creation of universal form of artistic situation, we will have to understand how *dhvani* comes to realise such a possibility. The primary part of this theoretical system meets the necessary requirements for laying down the aggregate structure for the creation, constitution, exposition and presentation of an ideal artistic situation, and accordingly, the ideal artistry is convincingly begotten in the division of the categories in the first place and the successful transformation in the second place. It is, indeed, the fixation of communication of both experiential and linguistic categories that finds out and establishes convincing groundwork for the acceleration of an artistic situation. In this way *dhvani* becomes a term for totality and the absolute in the artistic form, artistic structure and artistic manners.

III

In structuralist poetics, the conditions, circumstances, situations and events of creativity and ideal creativity are proposed and accepted to be observing a condition of both, division and revival, in terms of the constitution of the categories. For the matter of that, the end principle for such a purpose is believed to be the authority of confirmed evolution of language into meaning, or in other words, sensation into intellect. The major structuralists, beginning with Ferdinand de Saussure, Roman Jakobson, Roland Barthes, Gerard Genette and Greima, have substantiated the necessary framework for the whole situation. Especially it is Saussure who defines the perspective in which the structure of language could be stated to be a purpose and effect of finding a consequence when the last segments of relation, interrelation and inter-mediate relations are made to synchronise themselves along some universal coordinate(s). It is, thus, in structuralist style of constituting and comprehending an artistic situation that the categories, which evidently manifest as language and experience, are ultimately the main foundations of the significant system that in the later stage would emerge as a consolidated aggregate of great artistic situation. Language is a mass having an intensity to subjugate and correlate, divide and synthesise the several units simultaneously. For this reason, in any condition, the effect of language is contained in the independence and inter-dependence of the realistic division it brings about. For this reason sound, syntax, morphology, meaning and the sign situation could come to find a worth for structure that is so effectively a term for the whole debate. The expansion of language in the first place, in terms of the phonological performance and deviance must be a condition of recognition. Accordingly, Saussure would like to say that the generative principles of sound would ultimately present a rather consistent intention to harmonise meaning and other forms. The principal sounds like nasal, fricative, lateral, plosive and affricates have a manner of entering into obvious conjunction with parallel terms of induction, subsequently, the change in sound over a period of time would also mean a considerable change in meaning situation and consequently the grammatical function would also be equally affected. Yet, what would remain stationary and static would be the general configuration through which we come to know about the word as essentially being the word. This act of correspondence between two organic forms of wholesome categories would, therefore, be basically the events through which a proper understanding of language situation could be achieved. This would amount to saying that the correlative that unites sound as an object and sound as an event is the value that has realistically entered into the scheme of expansion since the varying periods of historical and cultural changes. This necessity of elevating sound units to the meaning-generating system is a remarkable contribution that Saussure has felt and observed. Sound is proportionally, and, even otherwise, always suggested in relative worth of the things. Thus the way of utterance is also creative of the imminent form for the sake of itself and in this form we can perceive the presence of a number of relative and contra-relative objects. Thus while thus the language is made to express the contents, the first remarkable projection would be immensely activated in the sound condition. The extension of the structure would be carried on through the other sets of division within the linguistic system, and, for the purpose, the next order is syntax. Syntax is the cumulative graph of a language and appropriates the range, order, motif and basic ethos of the words. Inasmuch as they are joined, enjoined, conjoined, and disjoined while they are displaced forward and backward or upward and downward and the linear arrangement of word order develops the suitability for an associative function in phonology, semantics or even morphology. For this reason, correct order would find a numerical applicability in correct value, which would in turn bring about adequate conceptual forms. Saussure and others have emphasised the necessity of having a sequence for the presentation of an order in such a way that order itself is distorted for the sake of some external or internal concepts. If the order is composed along similar lines, it would assume paradigmatic formation, while, if it is routed through vertical terms, it would definitely be syntagmatic situation. In the structuralist tradition, any situation that brings about replacement, placement or displacement, is liable to accelerate events of creativity so much so that the exact and appropriate form is obtained. A word is supposed to be both, the beginning and the end, of the functional order designed in the concerned situation. For this reason selection of a word and several words purposely build up a fine perspective in advancing the cause of coherence. This act, inadvertently, commutes two formal divisions at any point of time. In the first place, there is the combination of certain words and the meaning of combination would be taken up in the largest possible sense of the word. And, for that matter, it would mean transmutation. Accordingly, whatever words come into combination with each other, will carry the precision of values in such a way that the proximity would yield the correspondence, and correspondence would act up to facilitate the complete exchange of value terms and value methods. This could be seen to be one of the great experimental methods, devised nicely in structuralist tradition, and the real rationale of the situation could be comprehended by looking at the product consequence and concept consequence obtained at the core of the greatest intensity. The combination of the word is an effect of procedural change; therefore, the probability of conversion of a natural situation into any significant property, is excellently maintained. The characteristic of combination of certain words is to expound the necessary component for elevating the strength of transmutation under an ideal condition. This particular pattern is always being conceived and adopted. Similarly, opposed to this, there is another method by which qualitative change in the manner of conduction of the contents is brought about. This method is accordingly called selection. In the event of selection, words are intended to beget cognitive effects around them, and, because of this, extreme rationalisation of the inherent properties are extracted out of themselves. Saussure sees these two situations as being synchronic and diachronic. The act of selection could be manifold and in the various circumstances in which the event is expected to be accomplished — both synchrony and diachrony would enter into a formative sequence. The changing nature of the word, either phonologically and semantically or morphologically, would base an effect of change, and this would be included under the diachronic condition. Diachrony of the word is an important source of value generation and determines what semantic form the word is going to acquire. Sometimes, however, because of reversal in historical and sociological or cultural tendencies, the process of change does not coincide with any noteworthy formation of any property that could enlarge the structural foundation. Each of these, according to Saussure, is understood as synchrony. The exact examination of all the advertent formation must yield two results based on these correspondences via diachrony and synchrony. If the groundwork is associated with the time of stagnation in respect of the structure and sound, grammar, meaning, words and the like, then the assortment would become compulsive while the changes in structure are spread over a period of time and induce the fact of reference. It would definitely be assertive in both designation and affiliation to the greater and larger models of the artistic situation. The view of matter, being upheld by Saussure and others, seems to be fit for the sake of creating a homogeneous apparatus for initiating lengthened conceptual structures. Each such structure facilitates and removes the passive conditions and puts forth views for the creation of the absolute and proper orientation of the categories. The linguistic system or experiential foundation proposes the quality of definite and concrete expository variants inasmuch as every variant would signify and obtain perception and order. The necessity of such a unity of concept-forming terms brings about the recognition of structuralist interpretation of the artistry.

There are some other divisions within the linguistic foundation which propose concentrated perspective in assessing the real worth of the corresponding form and morphological suggestion, structural grammar and semantic disclosing and revealing of the identity of combination of experience and language comes up for observation and notice. In the constituent units, the grammatical categories will obviously play a role in their capacity as the sign or signifier. Similarly noun, pronoun, verb, adverb, proposition, gerund and infinitive, and all the phrases associated with the categories will bring forth association for adopting a scheme of expansion. In grammatical forms, the effect of insertion is understood in displacement and replacement of the unit that is intended/ procured. This has the potential of exacting optimum configuration for the sake of growth in the prescribed direction. Noun, for example, would become the best available means to interact and rotate and also revise the structure of all the associating forms. The role of grammatical categories is to develop strength in multiple divisions, which are intentionally and regularly brought about by the process of changes. The corollary to this advancement is seen in the way in which appropriate value terms are constituted leading to semantic universal. The nature of meaning in any circumstances is qualitative and thus meaning is formulated by the virtue of expository absolute in linguistic and experiential condition. To this end, association and correlation, presentation and exposition, modification and synthesis could be the occasions to invent certain linguistic properties of the meaning. In the structuralist terms, meaning is essentially a product, sequence and consequence of the evolutionary principle found in the realisation of combination as an effect. For this reason, word and feeling, thought and sensation, sensation and intellect, imagination and sentence would create worthy situations necessarily for purifying the event of meaning. It would sometimes be almost like a proposition or a formula to bring about two parallels as if opposed, for example, sensation and intellect must be seen in terms of a generative method, yet, on the other hand, we cannot deny that there might be the reduction of the content in the both, and, for the same purpose, opposition would be applied securely. The meaning generation is to be seen to be associated with the application of reasonableness and for this reason every meaning is considered to be created at the point of intersection or the point at which the product of combination and selection intersect each other. This point is also to be considered as the point where ideal sensibility is created. The ground of application of meaning intention and grammatical structure befits the result of transformation and marks an event in the progression of the artistry. Jakobson, Barthes and others have found a distinction between elevating significance of the word-order, purporting conjunction and secondary significance of meaning orientation bringing about universality to be concomitantly adjusted against each other, yet, however, in Saussure, the aspect of prolongation of combinatory events are more or less the accompaniments of similar magnitude in selectional context. The last significant division in this regard is supposed to be the compact network of sign system. In any linguistic form, the immensity of sign is obviously at the centre of structural focus. The event of sign is an order of equivalence or is obtained while the referential designation unequivocally situates a parallel term in other formation. The virtue of sign, according to Saussure is to rearrange, establish, reorganise and reassess every possibility for the elevation of the content. Thus, in sign, the methods are logically preparatory to the contentwise significance. In structuralist poetics, the dependence on sign, is, in fact, a process of reliance on the equation for the total effect. In this way, the concept of structure in any event is essentially one that encompasses every category involved in phonological, semiotic, morphological, syntactical and semantic universals and, the extent of analysis, under structuralist terms would effectively be a procedure to invent the methods of relationship and interrelationship conferred exceptionally by each on each.

IV

The formal methods applied in the structuralist poetics, for the sake of discovery of the events of creation and transformation of the linguistic and experiential categories, centre on a process of change, leading to creation of meaning through modification, synthesis resolution and finally evolution. In other words, the development of meaning is a situation that is firmly rooted in the procedure established in the unification, enrichment, concretisation refinement, precision, realisation and inculcation of the linguistic and emotive categories. It is appropriately an extraordinary event in which, in the first place, there is discovery of intending units and parts of the both linguistic and experiential models and once the units are discovered the procedures are laid down for the selection and combination of the parts. The summation of the whole into whole by virtue of constant evolution finally yields to meaning. The difference lies in the fact that the upgraded meaning is preceded by an actual network of differential values or, for that matter, is almost like a wave whose strength is not unified but is rather shared equally well by every single whole that constitutes the structure of the wave. The procedure of evolution and the factors leading to evolution could be grounded in the isolative variants purporting significance in the situation. For this reason, the division of linguistic and experiential categories into sign, signifier and signified as stages in the process of evolution is thoroughly justified. Sign constitutes a form in which all the units and parts of the given categories are correlated in the manner of a chain with one another. These units and parts, which correlate themselves and formulate finally the act of synthesis, are called signifiers. In an ideal condition when the medium, context and the content are finally adjusted within themselves so as to cause the generation of product of evolution bears the name of signified. It would mean that the number of individual words, letters, syllables, emotions, feelings have entered into the suitability of correspondence by the virtue of being morphologically, semantically, syntactically, semiotically and even otherwise, come together in view of similarities or differences in extraordinary historical, cultural or religious situations. This addition by the virtue of either opposition or difference could now become a movement in which there would be replacement and displacement at constant and regular intervals depending on the similar process of change in the historical and cultural situations. In the course of time, determinants would add to the purity of units and parts and a value that would sustain the adequacy of structure would appear and invariably effect the emergence of a proper interpretative consequence bearing the name of meaning would come up. While we proceed to understand the condition of meaning illustrated in the structuralist poetics, we are always reminded of the fact that every unit of a category, is, in fact, an opening for the sake of an admission to its own universal. After the initiation of the process when so many universals have gathered up, the reality of formation of an advanced concept would certainly be forthcoming. In the structuralist tradition, the process of causation is based on accumulation of expanded units obtained and achieved within the linguistic system, and once this has been obtained the consequent effect would be exactly consolidated in the aggregates of universals, produced immediately after the completion of the process. For the sake of this purpose, Saussure obtains distinct methods of transmutation of unit into the whole. For him, signifier is an object enlisted together through selection and every signifier configures identical sets of objects for the creation of concept. The primordial circumstances dealing with the purpose would certainly be the sound structure, and, at a later stage, each sound structure is converted into its equivalent for the scheme that is involved in this, is the gradual precision that is extended to both the primary and secondary structures, and at that the change of structure is coterminous with improvisation of the suppositional totality. The movement of the figures along such lines, assuredly begins at a time of organisation and precision in that every relative segment of terminal content has become a part of the largest universal. The intention of implanting a range and scale of meaning by mutating signifiers appears to be very unconventional, and, therefore modernist enterprise. It would, in the next place, mean that any situation, be it artistic, sociological, historical or religious could be defined and understood in terms of the distribution of the containing units within the categories, division of the same units understood in terms of progression and retrogration of the units, and finally, the organisation and reorganisation leading to the creation of complete effect from which we understand the emergence of value, in the first place, and meaning, in the second place. In the artistic perspective, procedure to canonise the grouping of symmetrical units and parts is a matter of the level of intensity that the linguistic or emotive categories would acquire. On the one hand, the social, cultural and religious circumstances, the division, distribution and organisation of the categories would depend on the bond of kinship, fraternity expressed in association, and cohesion characterised in the elementary form of conjunction. In each case, we can understand that the nature, form and function of structure are very important. Society has a structure in the form of the individuals who go on to make the laws of social causation; similarly, religion has its own structure in the manner of extension of myths and legends, which act as a binding authority on the individuals. The strengths of religion and society would be based on the fact that each of these structures has evolved into some kind of human value. Therefore, these are in a position to exert some kind of authority over the individuals. The parallel function of structuralist interpretation in these contexts would be to explore the signifiers through different kinship situations or mythological actions so that they may be added to yield to a complete and meaningful form which would ultimately lead to the creation of substantive meaning. In either of the situations, the division, distribution, organisation and evolution of the signifiers cannot be ruled out. The method of separation and isolation are actually added to discharge and perform the act of meaning-generation or value-orientation. For the purpose, Saussure is right when he says that value for a signifier could be fixed up when the underlying circumstance has emerged from a succession of the events. It is really a method of performance that brings forth the clarity of the conceptual arrangement. For this reason, sequence, order, graduation, chain, ladder, chronology, hierarchy and scale are supposed to be the initial conditionalities, whence we can have the beginning of an evolutionary process for the convergence of meaning in its primary as well as significant form. This appears to be one of the successful instruments of transformation modellised in structuralist poetics. While we proceed to understand Saussure, Barthes, Jakobson, Genette and Greimas, the emphasis has to be laid on trying to know under what exceptional circumstances each of these great theorists is engaged in finding a worth for resolution of an object into the event.

V

In *dhvani* and the structuralist poetics, the pursuit of organisation and the conduct of transformation of linguistic and emotive categories and subsequent emergence of an order of value and meaning could form a valid basis in advancing the terms of comparison to the absolutely universal standards. In *dhvani*, the magnitude of artistic effect and the configuration of an artistic product, both are reciprocal to each other, and for this reason when the exceptional enrichment in linguistic categories (*śabda, pada, varṇa, vākya*) and emotive models (*bhāva, vibhāva, anubhāva, sthāyībhāva, sañcārībhāva, ālambana, uddīpana*) is obtained, the process of idealisation is immediately facilitated. In this regard, it would be better to understand the utmost urgency in divising, explaining, exploring and comprehending the function of meaning that emerges as a result of the unification of every participating model and the category in the artistic situation. The earliest stages, in which the contents within the categories are specifically primordial, the achievement of the unified standard of composite valuation is something that is obtained right at the beginning of the situation. It is to be considered that the procedure to modellise and modify the category into one organised whole is brought about when placement of the content is in a sequence or an order suited to the diachronic mode of progression. Content situates the position for itself by entering into active conjunction with the other. The effect of conjunction rotates the cycle so harmoniously that extra covalence is created. The adequacy of this effect is germinated homogeneously for the sake of every other content that is expected to enter into the situation. When such a regrouping of several covalents is realised, we can easily understand how an ideal artistry is imminent. The categories in *dhvani* occupy place and position that might be multi-directional, yet when the higher intensity of enrichment has emerged, we have the possibility of presupposing that the transformation as such has taken place. The idea of transformation in this system is related to the creation of an ideal that has a definite role in the process of change of primary content/significant category/significant content. It must be stated with conviction that accomplishment of such a task is necessarily the addition of the terms of reality, reasonableness, elegance, purity, harmony and music to the primary contents and with the accession of these significances, the categories are finally assorted for the sake of universal condition. In *dhvani* theory, the idea of transformation is primarily brought about by addition, association, correlation, reduction, multiplication and the inverted expansion and also in some cases by division. The instrument of transformation suggests the inherence of absolute in each of such circumstances. The difference between the orthodox insignificance of the artistry and the conclusive significance of the newly born artistic situation is precisely hidden in the fact that, in the later stage, the precision, accuracy, appropriateness and the hardness of the artistic circumstances are conceived at the behest of the term of rationality. Now, everything could be seen in terms of a total, complete and indivisible formation of an event that is current, recurrent and concurrent, and every effect so produced is expressive of the reality of meaning. In *dhvani* there are both, the beginning and the end of the process of evolution, so much so that the expressive contents are at once modified into an assertive configuration, leading to an appropriate conclusive situation. The extent of change, manner of change, rate of change and the adequacy of change are necessarily the perfect formulations, which appear to create a sequence for the sake of inception and subsequent conjunction and comprehension of the creative categories. In structuralist poetics, the observation of the models and categories that could configure and invest themselves with the largest possible significance, is the genuine result and product of the growth of artistry. While the circumstances necessarily invent linguistic form (sentence, word, letter, and syllable) and emotive object (thought, experience, imagination), the worth of the underlying rationality could be seen in thoroughly codified and designated scale of value and meaning, emerging as a rule from such a situation. The question is necessarily only tentative as to how and why and when and where the correlation has effected the finality of transformation. What actually is worth noticing is only the range and length of concrete products intensifying universals and supra-universals in phonological, semantic, morphological, semiotic and syntactical foundations of the artistry. The growth of medium, context, and content assesses a corresponding complete growth of the categories like language and experience, therefore, the emergence of meaning carries an authenticity of quality. Exposition of system dealing with the nature, form, function and object of the meaning could be compulsorily assigned to the fact that the effect of correspondence, correlation, association could be successfully equated for the sake of high order of experiential and linguistic intensity. The measure of intention of the structure of the categories and subsequent division of the categories could enlist varieties of applicable models in social, religious and historical situations. Thus the essential merit of investigation into foundational significance of myth is well justified. It must be understood that myth is an amalgam of assured kinship structures in which the correspondence of object and subject is very important. The object is inverted to elevate the subject, and the subject is denoted to suggest the object. The inverse of such a correlation produces an order of significance that is described as myth. In structuralist tradition, the correspondence of myth with social, religious, historical structure is obviously what intends to examine as a part of something that would add and something that would distinguish the process of addition. Even otherwise, in *dhvani* system, the situation obtains a greater recognition in that it preoccupies with the essential understanding of the categorical structure beyond any immediate artistic form. Imminence of the methods of initiating the sequence of enriched contents to foresee the similarity of similar equivalents is, in fact, worth the pursuits of creation and composition of an ideal environment that works simultaneously with a focus on art and other variants of imitation like architecture, music, dance and painting. This would therefore form the acceptance of a common condition for convergence of the terms of comparison.

VI

In *dhvani* and the structuralist tradition, the constitution of the enriched categories and models validates the purpose of situating the instruments of metaphor as a principal object of causation. In *dhvani*, metaphor culminates the act of synthesis that has been underlying since the inception of artistry. In fact, the result of expanding the category is felt precisely in the graduation of medium, context, content and the models along the absolutes. For this reason, metaphor is both, the cause and effect of the acts manifested in multiplication, addition, association, conjunction, injunction, conception and inception. In structuralist poetics, the process of signification purporting a worth of value results into creation of conceptual forms with an ability to intercept the figurative and methodical signifiers. In this, therefore, the evolution of elementary linguistic models into their equivalent enriched conceptual forms would make the possibility of interpretation of value and meaning. This point of interception would ultimately evolve into comprehensive metaphor from which the universality of the situation would proceed. In both the situations, metaphor is conceived as an associative function, yet it enlarges afterwards into an independent body of figurative-rational and figurative-instrumental effects of perception. In either of the circumstances, the presentation of totality of meaning is obvious and well understood. As a point of native situation, there is primarily one concern of conceptualisation that could be intended at any point of time, and that is quite appropriately the event of generation of metaphor. Every metaphor finds a concrete worth in enhancing and expanding the rate of creation of precise contents which in turn brings forth the required connectivity to the larger artistic environment. This is to state, in other words, that, in metaphor the strength of form is so conspicuous that it immediately enacts the transmutation of an elementary and crude function into the authentic generation of the content. The metaphors, accordingly, have a basis in initiating the progression of the content both in the linear and cyclical positions. There might, however, be the differences in viewing the terms of metaphor with regard to the area of circumference created by the way of multiple association of the content. *Dhvani* system views the process as recurrent and universally inscribed while structuralist poetics approves only the present and the immediate location of the multiplicity of contents. Nevertheless, the transmutative condition of modification and resolution is the basis of processes that leads to the extension of the arguments in both the traditions.

VII

In *dhvani* and structuralist poetics, thus, the form and content congregate an urgency to conceive and procreate the linguistic and experiential categories so as to situate a term and condition of universality on rational principles. In each, the methodology of modifying an object into an event is operative formalistically and historically, and thus, we can understand the validity of purpose in opting for an exposition of all the valid events leading to the constitution of an ideal artistic situation.

1

Formal Methods I
Configuration and Organisation of the Categories

I

GENUINE artistic situation recognises and presupposes a manner of variation in the excellence of performable and non-performable categories that opt for a total and complete participation in the creation of an absolute artistic environment. The actual necessity for such an exercise could be variously described as synthesis, synchronisation, convergence, harmonisation, transformation and transmutation of the existing and received contents, and, for that matter, the operative condition in finding a meaning in terms of an idealised existence by implicated and explicated standards. The beginning of the whole event finds a concrete functional term by initiating a form of synthesis, and, to this extent, the specific event due upon language, thought, imagination, experience, *bhāva*, *sthāyībhāva*, *vibhāva*, *anubhāva* and *sañcārībhāva* along with *śabda*, *pada*, *varṇa* and *vākya* could be easily substantiated. The actual happenings of the series of events are sometimes perceived and sometimes indexed in the committed part of perception, and, for this reason, the entire configuration of artistry becomes enriched with those contents, constructs and categories which have meaning in terms of immediate as well as universal artistic performance. The methodical and methodological perception, involved in such an exercise, has been a matter of speculation in the Indian and the Western theoretical inquiries on the subject, and, therefore, the system of contemplation and investigation into the empirical configuration inherent upon idealised artistry has been brought about in the form of *dhvani* and structuralist poetics in Indian and the Western thought traditions respectively. Variables and coordinates, which tend to be the determinants of artistry, could be successfully explicated provided the nature of resolution of an object into event is accomplished with a graduated scale of committed and coherent ideology of transformation. This, in a way, would constitute one of the principles of assertion for the sake of the completion of the process of idealisation in artistry. It has to be understood that the receptive and communicative functioning of a category in an artistic form is subject to the corresponding strength of change that is to be introduced into the whole form in such a way that perceptible role is created by the aggregate of cumulative difference that would be seen or found between inter-spatial form of the structure of the categories. It would not be less than the required strength and the projected value of enrichment and independently or collectively a category has to function with regard to the prospective and formative sequence of actually conditioned and actually organised contents of the situation. On this account, we can understand that theoretical determination of the nature, form, object and functions of resolution is possible and we can also appreciate the inquisitive possibilities, which are open to speculation and mediation in *dhvani* and structuralist poetics in this regard.

II

Dhvani is an act of assertion of empirico-rational categories like language and experience which form an organised whole amongst all the known divisions, classification, attributes and aggregates of language and experience by an act of graduated and concentrated enrichment, refinement, idealisation and universalisation of the participating units of and parts of the respective categories.[1] The act of refinement invariably means the process of addition, multiplication, substraction in such a way that each is capable of forming both, injunction and conjunction, for the sake of an absolute and a concrete universal. The situation of interpretation would form a necessity of understanding of the structural formation and prospective synthesis of the coordinates which are specific to language and experience, and, for the purpose, we can conduct an examination of the situation by obtaining A and B as universals interposing value of significance under presented conditions and the progression of the variables along horizontal and vertical lines so as to successfully explicate an aggregate for the purpose.[2] For example; Σ is the aggregate and formation of synthesis would definitely invent the following equative form:

$$\Sigma = A + B$$

The seminal principle so adopted will further induce and configure the minor and major attributes having a progression

---

1. In the creation of *dhvani* the fact of evolution gains primary consideration inasmuch as every progression towards genuine formation accompanies the subsequent changes in structure and function of the categories. For further description on the subject, see Ānandavardhana:

   सर्वेष्वेव प्रभेदेषु स्फुटत्वेनावभासनम्।
   यद्व्यङ्ग्यस्याङ्गिभूतस्य तत्पूर्णं ध्वनिलक्षणम्।। – 2.33

2. The idea of transformation in the structuralist poetics is primarily the inculcation of value motif in the linguistic categories and as an imminent category to these emotive categories are procured for the sake of composite condition. For further description on the subject, see Jonathan Culler.

through the probability to enjoin a simultaneous effect, and, therefore, the arrangement will undergo a slight modification and change. In the following scheme, the explication of minor and major contents has been suggested:

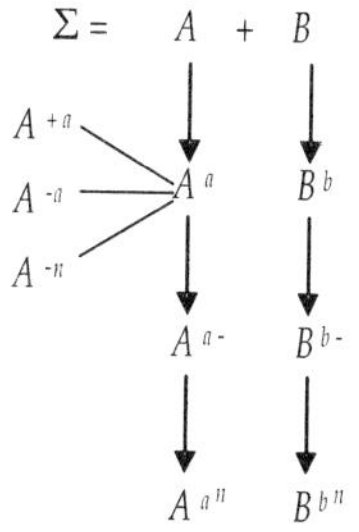

It is remarkable to understand that language and experience being situated and obtained in the form of *śabda, pada, varṇa,* and *vākya* and *bhāva, vibhāva, anubhāva, sañcārībhāva, ālambana* and *uddīpana* could come up for multiple distortions in the form of a synthesis for the sake of meaning. *Śabda,* for example, is capable of acquisition on three different occasions and different circumstances, and, for that matter, it could either enter into an addition or division or multiplication or even subtraction by the virtue of its primary strength that it derives from interacted cognition; hence, the result of expansion or deduction would be squarely generative of a universal in the form of meaning. Similar situation could be understood in respect of other categories like *pada, vākya, bhāva, vibhāva* and *anubhāva*. The earliest form of association that is evidently recognised, is the correspondence of one content with the others in a suitable medium and then context is established and, in the next place, the length of a content would accord a specific situation and form the category that tends to acquire certain benefits on account of its conclusive and assured enrichment. The continuity of situation is prolonged and sustained till the time one arrives at a complete convergence, right from the top of the artistic model to the bottom of the same model. In fact, it would be just better to say that graduation of the categories along a segmented triangular formation is obtained through a successive and repeated and corresponding replacement of one content by the other, another by yet another. Towards the close of the process every category and content is so purely idealised that absolute meaning is at once committed for the sake of advancement and expansion of a pure meaning. This, in fact, would make up the first important theoretical consideration with regard to the principle of *dhvani*. However, we can situate a parallel form of explanation by obtaining an equative urgency of the situation in the following manner:

$$\sum = A + \dot{A} + \dot{A} + \dot{A} + \dot{A} + \dot{A} + \dot{A} + \dot{A} + \dot{A}$$

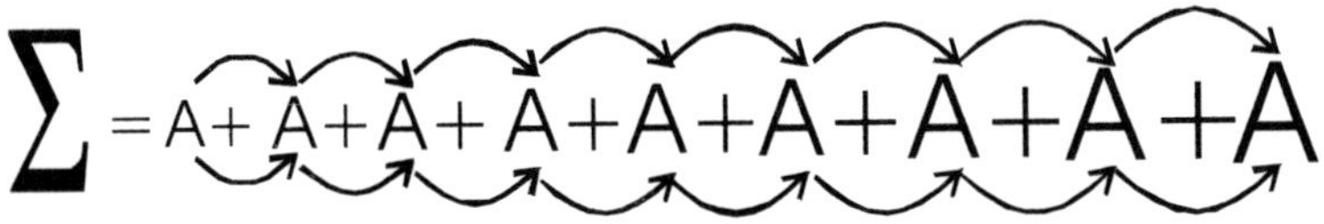

It can be seen that advancement and progression of content and categories generates both, the internal and external forms of enrichment, and therefore, expansion is assorted through the cumulative transfer of the internal content to the external content, and, for the same reason, every event of enrichment is succeeded by another and yet another and at the same time getting added to the another, thereby, at the end of the event the largest possible universal emerges, for which we can appropriate the name of *dhvani*. In *dhvani*, it must be suggested that consolidation and organisation of the event is prefixed by the actual working of *śabda, pada, varṇa, vākya, bhāva, vibhāva, sañcārībhāva, anubhāva, sthāyībhāva, ālambana* and *uddīpana* and thereby it would be worthwhile to consider the ideational circumstances attending the same order of conceptualisation. This foresees an assortment of a category in accordance with the intensity that it generates while modifying cause into effect, and, for that matter, *śabda* comes to preoccupy certain distinctive identities through which a successful completion of the process inherent to genuine artistry is intended.[3] *Śabda* is an identity of both, the function and order of the entire event in which determination of empirical form of language is, out of necessity, brought to realisation. It must be understood that the motif of order always takes precedence over the displacement movement of contents for stability and position. In fact, the content constituting the words, obtain compatability and liability for the sake of continuous movement towards the determination of an absolute in a form that has been proposed. The continuity of movement could be both reversible and irreversible, and, for that matter, the creation of optional condition is extended to every generative content presupposing a modification, constructed in every possible variety. The constituted propriety of the formal position occupied by *śabda* would make the situation of cause and effect possible. It would mean that any motif of value form induced by any content within *śabda* will have an equal opportunity of forming an association with nearly all the succeeding contents in the wholesome artistry. The idea of *śabda* being an object of modification, under reasonable and unreasonable circumstances, suggests the effective role performance through the subjection of complete content change by the power of extraordinary association generated by a function of revival of the longer form. In linguistic as well as emotive events, *śabda*, explicitly regulates the native and formal disintegration of the content thereby it has the capacity to include even the non-relative form of expression. The idea of *śabda* as an explicit generative unit could make out a case for

3. The conjunction of emotive situation with verbal antecedent could be taken to be as the substance of excellence in the creation of strength in the artistry. For further description on the subject, see Bharatamuni:

सच्चिदानन्द विभवात्सकलात्परमेश्वरात्।
आसीच्छक्तिस्तो बिन्दुर्विन्दोर्नाद समुद्भवः।। – 2

continuity of interpretative and consequential configuration of any model that comes off in the form of an equivalent. The expressed conjunction obtained via injunctive interpretation recorded to by the *śabda* retains the highest probability of movement in a given context and medium and for this reason no condition is merited as value proposition till the process of alliance and association has uniformly been stabilised, while, on the other hand, the consequential terms of expression are made active and functional through an indication of value at every recognised coordinate of progression. *Śabda*, for that matter, becomes an event in which intensity is both obtained and recognised so that all the external and all the internal terms of variation of value are concentrated and fixed till the time an absolute or the universal is created. Pāṇini considers the property of *śabda* as being additive and interrogative in exposing and maintaining synthesis as a necessary principle, while Patañjali, on the other hand substantially differs from the idea and says that *śabda* does not express or maintain any continuity whatsoever, and, for this reason, there is a dispersion of the absolute and the universals, and accordingly, concrete terms are invented in the graduation of transformation divided into several stages. This could, in turn, make out a case for the identity of *śabda* as being clearly marked out and authoritatively indexed as predominantly functional inasmuch as the operative content, the exposed content and the communicative content of *śabda* cohere around one principle form and through which transformation is initiated. There can be as many models and as many terms to approve a figure of coherence in which content of *śabda* is organised with an arrangement of the forms. The excess of synthesis or displacement cannot withhold any part of contextual motion, and, for this reason, Patañjali's perception of appearance seems to be quite logical. A *śabda* can form a unity and the length of such a unit will prescribe or exclude non-reversible forms of the other categories, which do not extend relative property to the other constituents. On this account, it would further be quite right to put a remark that the inductive and deductive intention approach and fix up a series of value events thus the nature of modification is assorted with an actual meaning of the proposed terms. There can be an inventory of logic that can be described through the following arrangement of the variables:

$$B = A_{\begin{smallmatrix} a^{+} \\ a^{-} \\ a^{+} \end{smallmatrix}} \; B_{\begin{smallmatrix} b^{+} \\ b^{-} \\ b^{+} \end{smallmatrix}} \ldots\ldots\ldots \; N_{\begin{smallmatrix} n^{+} \\ n^{-} \\ n^{+} \end{smallmatrix}}$$

The description of probable expansion of a *śabda* makes it possible to find out a description through multiple variable arrangements in which extension of one factor elevates the enrichment capacity of a particular content by juxtaposing the distribution through additive properties. For that matter, we can understand that strength of factor is obtained along all the possibilities of addition as suggested by the above equation. Under the unusual circumstances *śabda* conducts an exclusive property of the division of enrichment in which an observer's capacity to realise is divided into threefold universals in the form of significant realisation, signified realisation and significative realisation. Bhartr̥hari, in fact, makes mention of the idea that the origin of *śabda* is conditionally rooted in the reinvention of a factor in infinity or even the continuity of addition towards a factor in infinity. Thus, he makes the condition of inquisitive reality to be the necessary part of the exposition of *śabda* as a principle of enrichment of transformation. Accordingly, it might appear as if a *śabda* continues to obtain and create a unit of the content or the contents themselves while still the immediate compulsive order has ceased to operate. Bhartr̥hari opts for an associative function by repeatedly investing the entrance of *śabda* into the local as well as the universal order, hence, the stretch of a proposition being carried by a *śabda* becomes evident even in a non-spatial environment. It would be quite interesting to find out how the general and the exclusive properties of the *śabda* are intentionally cognised with an optimum probability of enrichment, for this reason, individual conjunction and universal index of *śabda* are absolutely perfect.

III

In *dhvani, śabda* constitutes a primary goundwork for the intention and commitment for a systematic and organised synthesis of the participating categories. The method for the completion of an exercise is correspondence and mutation. At the beginning, there is an identification of aggregate properties and once the act of identification is complete, the validity of assortment is established as a rule; for example, the continuation of the manner of reassessment of *bhāva, sthāyībhāva* along with *śabda* and *pada* is to be brought to the extreme level of value-generation. There is a certainty in finding mutual, complimentary and continuous replacement of the contents of the categories through an exclusive, interactive dispensation. For this reason, the correspondence of *A* with its supplementary variants *A* would be by adding the associative factors through a continuous replacement of non-associative factors till the time a complete change in the length of association is fixed and expressed. Ānandavardhana in *Dhvanyāloka* could understand how the situation marks an event in the growth of artistry:

> यथा पदार्थद्वारेण वाक्यार्थः सम्प्रतीयते।
> वाच्यार्थपूर्विका तद्वत्प्रतिपत्तस्य वस्तुनः।। – 2.10
>
> *yathā padārthadvāreṇa vākyārthaḥ sampratīyate*।
> *vācyārthapūrvikā tadvatpatipattasya vastunaḥ*।।

The form of comprehension purported through the word obtains a realistic invention of complimentary model at the tertiary level and to commute this invention of appropriate value, there is a formal association of the active contents within the *śabda* with the inclusive conjunction in the external environment of the artistry. The purpose of making an expressive form would primarily be to reciprocate an assertive expression in all the categories. *Śabda* invents a possibility of cumulative refinement by inverting the length of value, and, on that account, the value becomes most suitable to the realistic growth of artistry. Ānandavardhana's insistence on having *śabda* as a model presents several new developments in the idea of suitability and appropriateness of a category to the constructs. There is explicit evidence to point out that the enrichment of a *śabda* in the capacity of a model and the assorted refinement of the same as a category are synchronised along a point of deception where the authority of construction of appropriate linguistic forms becomes quite realistic. To this extent, one understands how the progress of *śabda* by inducting logical continuity and also by enlarging the length of aggregate object, are primarily the tools for the creation of a larger system of meaningfulness, so as to introduce a specific content to the medium. The acceptance of *śabda* as a significant, ideational and ideological formation is generally a pre-condition for obtaining excellence in poetic composition. Bharatamuni adopts and includes deduction while justifying how the *śabda* could form a primary ground for the initiation and growth of an artistic situation. In the *Nāṭyaśāstra*, a distribution between an appropriate *śabda* and an ideal *śabda* is maintained accordingly, as each constructs the objects of correlation between the context and the medium. There can be no deviance in assessing the probability of a selection of a *śabda* on account of its induction into the generic system, while, on the other hand, the movement of *śabda* towards the original point of refinement continues. To constitute significance in artistry there will have to be a motivation in the participating category, and to accomplish the situation, there is a regular and continuous intra-transformation of *śabda* via the relative contents that come nearer on account of the specific value generated by the *śabda*. In Bharata's view *śabda* has the strength of initiating multiple divisions within the associative functions of other contents of the artistic situation. It has to be accepted that the extent to which and the amount for the sake of which *śabda* has injuncted the association, would simply have to further the enrichment of the situation. It would be apparent that *śabda* is precisely both, the form and event, in such a way that its associative value and the idealised value are almost at par with the intensity of refinement. Even in the Alaṁkāra tradition, the propensity of *śabda* to build up an attitude and conviction for the sake of extra- and intra-inversion is clearly substantiated. Bhāmah could elucidate the conviction by suggesting that the repeated, regular and multiple variations in *śabda* interact and thereby support the methodological strength in the assertive part of the situation. Thus, *śabda* is both, logical at the beginning and a necessary cause for the overall comprehensibility. The actual effects, which come to be exposed for the association, are the stability acquired by the idealised part of a *śabda* and the concentration of and extended generative possibility. For this reason Abhinavagupta, Kuntaka, Mahimabhaṭṭa and even Dhanañjaya have insited upon an extra-effective universality to be the necessary conjunction for all situations. It would mean that the ideal part of the *śabda* would be specific for the absolute transformation, hence, Ānandavardhana suggests that the strength of a word is built around the preceding and succeeding urgency of forceful context, medium and content. These make the situation in *śabda* to be a necessity for desirable changes in content, configuration and the formal structure of the artistry.

The necessity of an ideal artistic situation could advance and presuppose an exact and concentrated form of *pada* and *vākya*. *Pada* is a beginning of the process of reasonable and confirmed revival of the strength of designated group of words in terms of its proposition and value. In fact, it is better to say that the process of revival of an identified *śabda* grows and even continues till the time there is an organisation of structure of values for the sake of creative strength in the functioning of the whole linguistic situation by the standards of constitutive urgency. There cannot be any presupposition through an individual *śabda* or group of *śabda* just for the reason that the native property of *śabda* focuses the merit of proposition not by the immediate significance but by the collective significance acquired through stable, fixed and effective correspondence under different contexts and situations. To view *pada* as a consciously developed formula for inculcating an effect of interpretation of value, one will have to record that the displacement of consequential event, lending to a formulaic structure of committed interrelation within the varying meaning, logically includes a framework and opening for reassessment at various levels, and, simultaneously, at various devisions. It is quite fascinating to know that Bhartṛhari presupposes chronological introduction of the formal contents of the *śabda* in association, and, for this reason, the completion of the event of association would take up a long but assured emergence in the form of meaning. Even Pāṇini could subscribe to this very idea and suggests a complete modification when the index and length of value of the words in association could accrue simultaneously and embody an idealised formation through a large communicative form spread over an entire segment of the unit. What actually happens is that the ability to create a method of correspondence tends to be greater in those *śabda*s which open themselves for communicative facility at the instance of a large-scale mutation of the contents within. This makes the whole constructs open for an optimum enrichment. Ānandavardhana considers the situation to be very specific and quite necessary for exposing the content of *pada* both for internal and external communication. In internal communication, the primary function of *pada* is supposed to be the alignment and coordination of the creative contents along an assorted chain of events, and, for that matter, it could presume an absolute synthesis through the variables included in the value concentrated coordinates. This fact conceives another possibility through the action created on account of excessive reversibility of the lengthened contents and the insistence on comprehending a variety of concomitant facts for the production of an ideal manner of synthesis. This idea is enlarged in the following verses of Ānandavardhana's *Dhvanyāloka*:

> रसाभावतदाभासतत्प्रशान्त्यादिरक्रमः।
> ध्वनेरात्माङ्गिभावेन भासमानो व्यवस्थितः।। – 2.3
>
> *rasābhāvatadābhāsatatpraśāntyādirakramaḥ*।
> *dhvanerātmāṅgibhāvena bhāsamāno vyavasthitaḥ*।।

In this, we can understand that the effective conjunction obtained by explicating the intended modification through gradual, systematic and confirmed changes in the configuration in such a way that the each configuration is absolute of the whole. This makes the imminence of primary artistic situation intentionally concrete because of the fact that independent as well as relative positions accupied by the categories are clearly defined. In Ānandavardhana's understanding, the occasion of pure artistry is a continuous development of the movement of contents towards an end. The idea of synthesis proposed as a rule finds approval in Abhinavagupta, Mammaṭa and Rājaśekhara. In Abhinavagupta's view, the presentation of linguistic categories for the sake of an association in an artistic medium calls for a major change in both the structure and function of the participating models.

The characteristics of change must precisely be associated with the direct assortment of meaning generating strength through actual injunctions so that the emergence from a primary situation would comply with the creation of extra-rational figures. Similarly, Rājaśekhara conceives proportion and order in properly distinguishing the functional categories from the non-functional categories, and therefore, he classifies the relative worth in accordance with the strength generated in *mati, buddhi,* and *āhārya*. Mammaṭa, on the other hand, could interpret the situation through finding the worth of cognition in the individual references created by the denotation of the word and the suggestivity that is normally brought about by an explication of the same reference in individual or associative context. For Ānandavardhana, the conception of *pada* would become significant where situative strength is exactly incorporated with a larger interpretative significance, and, for that matter, the process of induction begins right at the moment in which the word is brought to fixation in an external environment.

It is now possible to find out the meaning of association that leads to creation of *dhvani* principle in artistry by adopting the following equative arrangement:

$$\delta=\Sigma+\pi+\theta$$

In which Σ is variable conjunction

π is variable injunction

θ is variable comprehension

This equation would sum up the consequence of acquired meanings in every environment, and, accordingly, it could also be comprehended that the actual nature of model creation, category construction and content formation in rendering of synthesis in δ justifies the virtue of association in which every content is upgraded with noteworthy enrichment and proceeds to fix up universal synthesis in Σ, π and θ, facilitating the creation of *dhvani* as a principle.

The growth of an absolute form in artistry develops remarkable varieties of conjunction in which *vākya* appears to be very important. *Vākya* is an object of concentrated organisation of thoroughly cognised models of interpretative inquisition in such a way that projection of the content is equal to the reception of the content and both the facilities are extended to revive expressive association cyclically or otherwise. *Vākya* injuncts the principle of modification through specific changes brought about in the elementary structural set-up of the *śabda* and *pada*, and, because of this, the primary openings at the centre of reversibility are obtained on account of a transition that the inclusive forms may make within the proposed limit.[4] The existence of *śabda* or *pada* in a *vākya* would ultimately lead to the formation of designated universals, for example, if Σ is the *vākya*, it would facilitate the lengthening of primordial *śabda A* by distorting the supplementary functions or correspondence and inversion to the extent that *śabda A* is indexed as a figure of potential suggestive marker. Similarly, it would also include the natural supplements and fractions of *B* till the time the process of inversion is revived through the stretch of absolute modification into a proposition. This ability to offer inclusive categorisation would be extended to other similar parts so that an authoritative version of universal is directly obtained. Bhartṛhari expounds the principle and finds an inquisition by stating that every regular turn in the position of word presupposes an order in universality, and, therefore, both the *śabda* and *pada* are conjoined through a conjugal principle to select and achieve a turn when the context and

4. The incident of linguistic universalisation through upbringing of *śabda*, *pada* and *vākya* is a matter of great significance in the creation of *dhvani*. For further description on the subject, see Ānandavardhana:

   अविवक्षितवाच्यस्य पदवाक्यप्रकाशता।
   तदन्यस्यानुरणनरूपव्यङ्ग्यस्य च ध्वनेः।।
   यस्त्वलक्ष्यक्रमव्यङ्ग्यो ध्वनिर्वर्णपदादिषु।
   वाक्ये सङ्घटनायां च स प्रबन्धेऽपि दीप्यते।। – 3.1, 2

the medium are properly inclined to receive the contents directly and convincingly. Even Pāṇini could comprehensively approve the functioning of the composite *vākya* by developing a model for the purpose in which additive properties of the *śabda* and *pada* have been derived from the highest order of enrichment. Accordingly, Ānandavardhana considers *vākya* to be a complete form of expression that is located in the extreme of the point of synthesis, modification, change and resolution, and, for that matter, all the effect of assertion is derived from the exact logic of presentation. The expansion of the constituents like *śabda* and *pada* could be brought about by advancement of the positive and also by exchanging the enriched unit. On the whole, Ānandavardhana could consider the prospect of modification of *vākya*, *śabda* and *pada* simultaneously and conjointly and in which the primary effect of expression is supposed to be higher than the secondary motif of resolution. It would now convey the idea that the interrelationship between *śabda*, *pada* and *vākya* progresses towards resolution only when external factor like context and internal events, like the medium and the content, are symetrically conceived, and exactly because of this, creation of *dhvani* becomes possible. Ānandavardhana in *Dhvanyāloka* develops this idea and comprehends a variety of functional forms appearing to justify the situation:

> वाच्यवाचकचारुत्वहेतूनां विविधात्मनाम्।
> रसादिपरता यत्र स ध्वनेर्विषयो मत: ।। – 2.4

> *vācyavācakacārutvahetūnāṁ vividhātmanām* ।
> *rasādiparatā yatra sa dhvanerviṣayo mataḥ* ।।

The ideal form of an artistic situation would be a definite event with regard to the fact that active contents creating a suitability of substance and extraordinarily active form bringing about a rationalisation of the content are associated in a homogeneous equilibrium.[5] This equilibrium gives strength to the presentation of the wholesome form to the external world. In this regard, at least, one important condition is obtained and that is related to the direct observation, comprehension and visualisation of the independent situations through an exact, accurate, concrete form of total judgement related to the classificatory and divisible contents lying within the form of reception. The quality of communication and association brought about by the regular displacement of contents makes it possible for any empirical situation to generate maximum response to the external situation. In fact, it would be better to suggest that several openings which are possible to be created in *vākya* for the sake of the assignation of maximum value to minor constructs is a characteristic of the progress of *vākya* towards universality. This condition is obtained as a proportionate function to the larger artistic circumstances attending the creation of a situation. There can be at least certain exclusive necessities that we can induct into the meaning of a particular form of an ideal framework. Ānandavardhana, for this purpose, suggests that the extent of displacement must produce a model of transformation and for that matter the substitution and intra-substitution of *śabda* and *pada* will similarly produce empirical forms of creativity.

In *dhvani* system the theoretical function and applicational necessity of enriching the attending models are so well presented and justified that the artistry culminates into induction and deduction of the categories. Ānandavardhana

---

5. *Dhvani* as an instrument of modification presupposes a thoroughgoing resolution of every event associated the formation of an artistic event. It is thus simultaneity of convergence that has to introduce significance everywhere. For further description on the subject, see Ānandavardhana:

उक्त्यन्तरेणाशक्यं यत्तच्चारुत्वं प्रकाशयन।
शब्दो व्यञ्जकतां बिभ्रद्ध्वन्युक्तेर्विषयी भवेत।। – 1.15

foresees the entire framework through a methodical substitution that is obtained amongst *bhāva, sthāyībhāva, vibhāva, anubhāva* and *sañcārībhāva*. In each, the formation of active content and communication of activated context could be understood to be maximum, and therefore, the emergence of concrete universal or absolute on account of modification of each into each is a reality. *Bhāva* could be found to be an inclusive category, that, in itself, is permanently assorted and brings about the positional and situational placement of the contents. Bharatamuni considers this property of *bhāva* to be exceptionally idealised, and therefore, understands that the formal function of *bhāva* is to substantiate an index or fixed yet absolute adaptability to the artistry.[6] Later theoreticians like Bhāmah, Abhinavagupta, Mammaṭa, Kuntaka, Rājaśekhara, Dhanañjaya, Vāmana and Paṇḍitrāj Jagannātha have examined the structural situation of *bhāva* and accordingly have ascribed nine predominant indices of universality to it. These stages are the following:

1. *Śṛṅgāra*	4. *Raudra*	7. *Bībhatsa*
2. *Hāsya*	5. *Vīra*	8. *Adbhuta*
3. *Karuṇa*	6. *Bhayānaka*	9. *Śānta*

In each of these idealised functional forms, the necessity of

6. The significance of order suggests the strength of enrichment, hence transformation. Bharatamuni ascribed a due recognition to the idea by speaking of inter, intra and intermediate transformation. Among the succeeding theorists, order was almost entirely the concept initiating the formation of an ideal medium and an ideal context. Bhāmaha, Vāmana, Ānandavardhana, Abhinavagupta, Mammaṭa and Rājaśekhara have consolidated the actual systematisation by speaking of the actual relevance in having the worth of enrichment. For further description on the subject, see Bharata:

यथा बीजाद्भवेद् वृक्षो वृक्षात्पुष्पं फलं यथा।
तथा मूलं रसाः सर्वे तेभ्यो भावा व्यवस्थिताः॥ – 6.38

external and internal division is brought to a clear and concrete representation through the application of specific value order for each. The value orders create very coherent and harmonious models of performance by synthesising quite logically the native content with external object. In this regard, it is worthwhile to make mention of the fact that in an artistic situation that tends to come out of the purity of rationalised form is constantly changed to promote the virtue of an action lying in the native situation. *Bhāva* generally is a figure of action and continuity of action in such a way that primary basis of action is codified. It can be understood that the event in which the extent of artistry is reduced to non-native forms the role played by *bhāva* becomes very important. It can create a formal basis for communication between various segments of the artistry, and, for that matter, there is a chain of invented communicable objects focusing and forming comprehensible sequence of the rationalised contents so necessary to bring about strength in the artistry. There could also be another function that is equally important and that is the induction of the content at every significant modalisation and value. This helps in associating greater or smaller scales of enrichment in the object being signified.

*Sthāyībhāva*s, in the next place, could be seen to be as the predominant part of an infinite yet constantly recurring states of experience that are projected and synthesised through an independent functional form leading to the creation of an exact and unchangeable model of an experience like *bhāva*. *Sthāyībhāva*s are also nine in number which could be mentioned as:

1. *Rati*	4. *Krodha*	7. *Jugupsā*
2. *Hāsa*	5. *Utsāha*	8. *Vismaya*
3. *Śoka*	6. *Bhaya*	9. *Sama*

*Sthāyībhāva*s constantly affect the motif of an artistic situation by granting a form of irreversibility so that the content could operate upon exclusive length of the medium so as to make it absolute in itself. By the standard of action, the resoluble part of *sthāyībhāva* remains purposely so concrete that the consequence of resolution does not affect the presentation of facts and because of this the positive terms and the negative terms do not enter into any form of change whatsoever through recurrence of arrangement and rearrangement. This could be seen as one of the occasions to find out the validity of conceptualisation. There are other important structures involved in the process of creation of an artistic situation, which could be categorised as *vibhāva*, *anubhāva* and the *sañcārībhāva*. The important function that the categories perform is that they invent the act of communication of an experience to internal artistic environment (*vibhāva*) by promoting and devising certain objects to constitute the chain of events (*ālambana* and *uddīpana*).[7] On other occasions, the event of communication is externalised inasmuch as the external experience has to be conveyed to the external world and the process is completed by these empirical forms which communicate emotion to the external world (*anubhāva*). While constantly filling in and replacing weaker parts of experience with more enriched forms *sañcārībhāva*s keep up the necessary strength of artistry. The process of creation of a gap and its subsequent filling in is so massive and rampant that it is immediately turned into a universal. The entire structure could be graphically presented in the following manner:

---

7. Formation of emotive significance in the manner of *bhāva, vibhāva, anubhāva, sañcārībhāva* is itself expressive of the beginning of the process of ratiocination. In that the manner of exposition is itself absolutely concerete. For further description on the subject, see Ānandavardhana:

रसाभावतदाभासतत्प्रशान्त्यादिरक्रमः।

ध्वनेरात्माङ्गिभावेन भासमानो व्यवस्थितः।। – 2.3

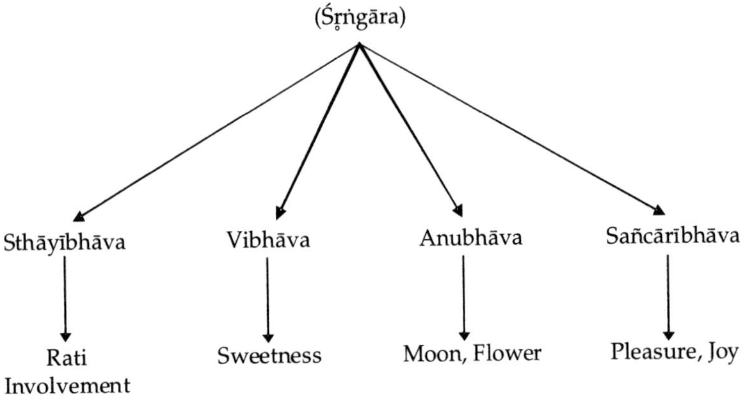
(Śṛṅgāra)
Sthāyībhāva
Vibhāva
Anubhāva
Sañcārībhāva
Rati
Involvement
Sweetness
Moon, Flower
Pleasure, Joy

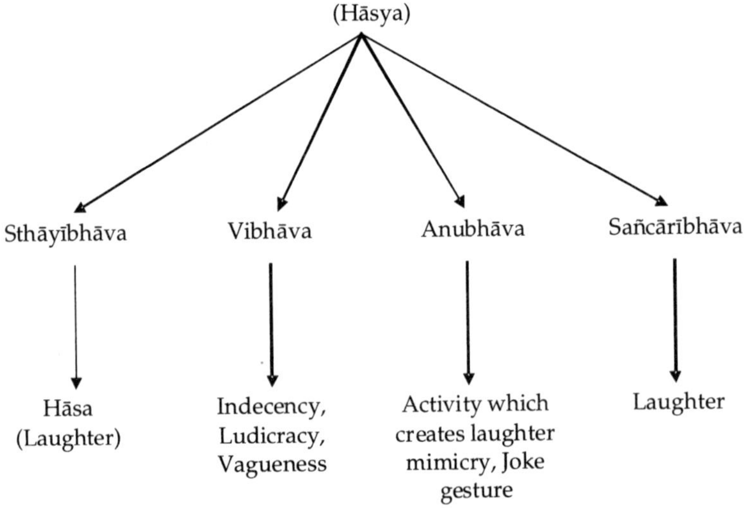
(Hāsya)
Sthāyībhāva
Vibhāva
Anubhāva
Sañcārībhāva
Hāsa
(Laughter)
Indecency,
Ludicracy,
Vagueness
Activity which
creates laughter
mimicry, Joke
gesture
Laughter

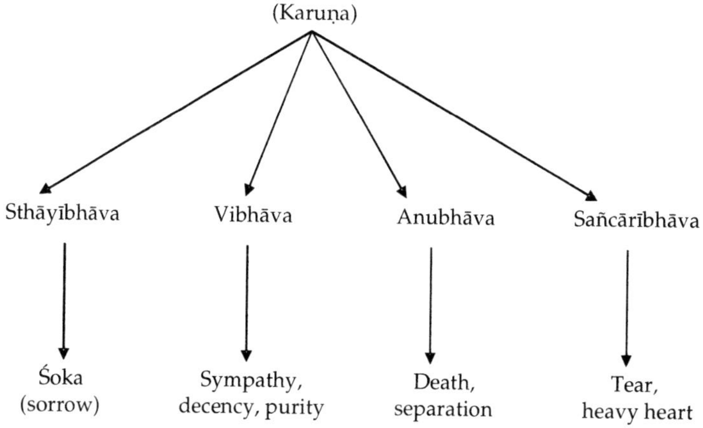
(Karuṇa)
Sthāyībhāva
Vibhāva
Anubhāva
Sañcārībhāva
Śoka (sorrow)
Sympathy, decency, purity
Death, separation
Tear, heavy heart

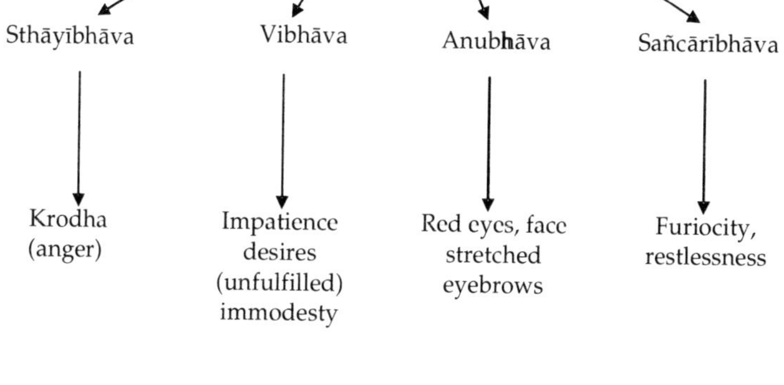
(Raudra)
Sthāyībhāva
Vibhāva
Anubhāva
Sañcārībhāva
Krodha (anger)
Impatience desires (unfulfilled) immodesty
Red eyes, face stretched eyebrows
Furiocity, restlessness

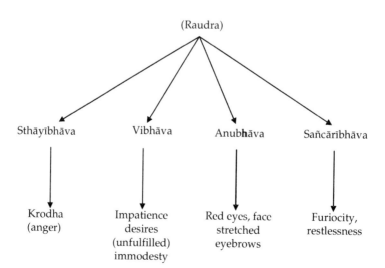

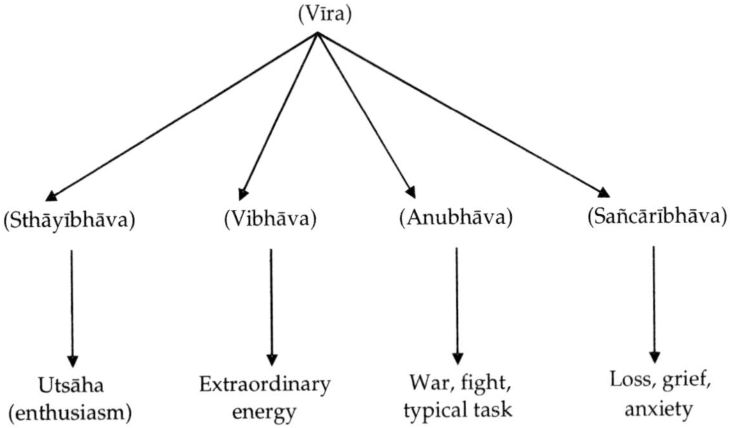
(Vīra)
(Sthāyībhāva)
(Vibhāva)
(Anubhāva)
(Sañcārībhāva)
Utsāha (enthusiasm)
Extraordinary energy
War, fight, typical task
Loss, grief, anxiety

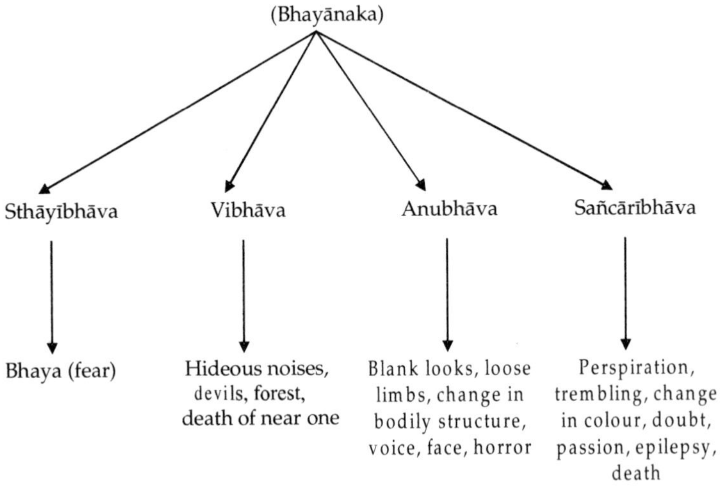
(Bhayānaka)
Sthāyībhāva
Vibhāva
Anubhāva
Sañcārībhāva
Bhaya (fear)
Hideous noises, devils, forest, death of near one
Blank looks, loose limbs, change in bodily structure, voice, face, horror
Perspiration, trembling, change in colour, doubt, passion, epilepsy, death

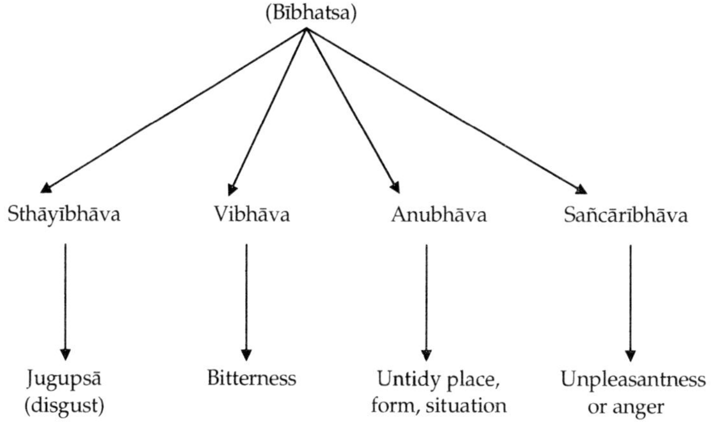
(Bībhatsa)
Sthāyībhāva
Vibhāva
Anubhāva
Sañcārībhāva
Jugupsā (disgust)
Bitterness
Untidy place, form, situation
Unpleasantness or anger

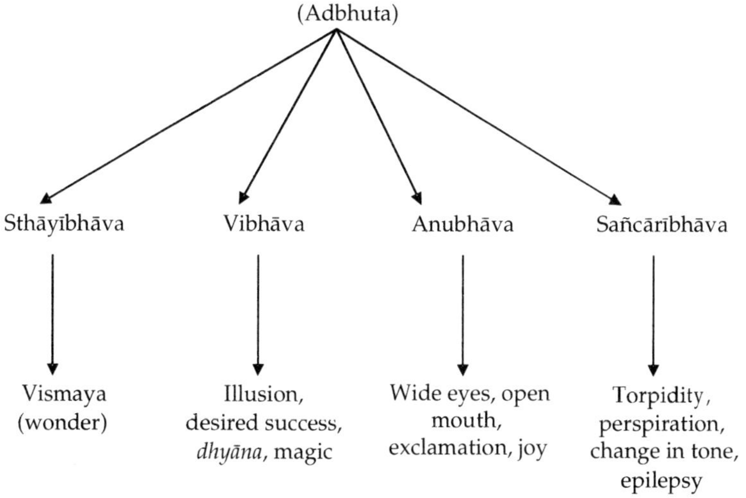
(Adbhuta)
Sthāyībhāva
Vibhāva
Anubhāva
Sañcārībhāva
Vismaya (wonder)
Illusion, desired success, *dhyāna*, magic
Wide eyes, open mouth, exclamation, joy
Torpidity, perspiration, change in tone, epilepsy

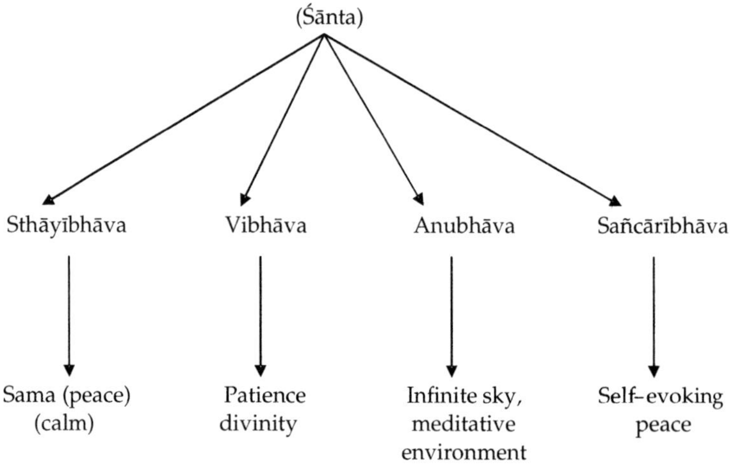

The concentration of generative categories and subsequent expression of absolute form anticipate the creation of recognisable and identifiable textuality of the creation and could be primarily denoted by the facts of excessive rationalisation and purer linguistic orientation.[8] In *dhvani* system, the artistry contained in a text is supposed to be primarily of three types. In first place, the contents of the forms are refined and enriched so much so that the act of enrichment brings about a total revision of the situation. Secondly, the act of correspondence and identification of appropriate contents do not stay back as a model to supplement the situation with an additional strength. This intermediate order of artistry is supposed to be somewhat inferior to the earlier one, hence, it is not admitted to the level of great artistry and finally there is also the third category in which models and categories do not respond to the qualitative enrichment, thus the poetic situation emerges to

8. The primordial forms remain the foundations of a great artistic formation. Thus, language that sustains the adequacy of the context will be a fit model for evolution. For further description on the subject, see Saussure.

be without any authenticity of contents. In these three variants of textuality, the proposition of assessment, revival, invention and reinvention are constantly brought to mutation in such a way that the expressed content, presented content and communicated content are realistically resolved and factually determined. In the first form, the authority of invention of a category (*śabda, pada, bhāva, vibhāva, sthāyībhāva, sañcārībhāva,* and *anubhāva*) is subject to an extraordinary shift in the act of correspondence between one category and the other, for example, *bhāva* is an opening for further terms in enrichment only through the proximity of *śabda* it could have at the given period of the time. Similarly, other categories also indicate models of preference for obtaining a worthy position in the hierarchy constituted for the pupose. It must be understood that mutation and correspondence bring forth a distinct and designated sequence in such a way that the beginning leads to an end and the end is recreated in the beginning. The following situation is conveyed by the interpretation that we would like to put forth:

Bhāva		
↓		*Anubhāva*
Śabda		↑
↓		*Śabda*
Sthāyībhāva		↑
↓		*Sthāyībhāva*
Pada		↑
↓		*Pada*
Vibhāva		↑
↓		*Bhāva*
Vākya		↑
↓		*Śabda*
Sañcārībhāva	→	↑

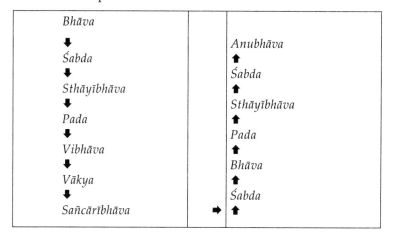

It could now be understood as to how functionality in appropriate order of universality could be comprehended and substantiated in each of the cases. The presentation of the active part of the content is to be brought about with such a great speed that the magnitude of function is almost equal to the concentration of the contents. Therefore, the principality of refinement is almost certainly a fact in the whole process of comprehension. There could be another way of strengthening the imminent assimilation of active categories into active categories through direct modification, for example, *vibhāva* could approach a modification through a *śabda* provided the intensity of content in *vibhāva* is proportionately equal to that in *śabda*. *Dhvani* always gets a rational version of the forms which are involved in the process and for this reason at any point of time there can be four important variants of external environment: (1) absolute, (2) universal, (3) rational, (4) suprarational and in these modes of function of artistry, the event of *dhvani* is completed.

In the first place, as we can see how the act of functionality resolves the largest condition of comprehensibility and realisation directed towards the assimilation of external and internal situations. The outward growth of the content in *dhvani* acquires a specific feature in substantiating the former conditions. This ensures the constant interplay of the categories so as to borrow a quality of thought from the act of comprehension. Ānandavardhana considers the arrangement of *śabda* and other constructs in a composite situation in such a way that every subsequent event is full of the explicated variants. The performances of category, say for example, *anubhāva* that is placed within the evolutionary system can have multiple fractions just to associate itself with the next advancing or descending form. The question deserves to be asked as to what comes in consequence of the sudden manifestation of resolvable parts against the irresolution of the preceding situation. Ānandavardhana has considered the question and suggested an answer in the form of the juxtaposition of object and subject through cognised interpretative object to which both the object and the subject must intentionally embody themselves. Ānandavardhana's *Dhvanyāloka* expresses the situation in the following terms:

न चायमलक्ष्यक्रमव्यङ्ग्यस्यैव ध्वनेर्विषयः।
यतो यत्र साक्षाच्छब्दनिवेदितेभ्यो विभावानुभावव्यभिचारिभ्यो
रसादीनां प्रतीतिः, स तस्य केवलस्य मार्गः। – 2.22

na cāyamalakṣyakramavyaṅgayasyaiva dhvanerviṣayaḥ ।

yato yatra sākṣācchabdaniveditebhyo

vibhāvānubhāvavyabhicāribhyo rasādīnāṁ pratītiḥ, sa tasya kevalasya mārgaḥ ॥

It is to be understood that the sequence and arrangement of *śabda*, *pada* and *vākya* on the one hand, and *bhāva*, *vibhāva* on the other, should comprehensively substantiate the position and sequence of explicated and implicated content in such a way that proper assimilation could be made and the excellence of artistic situation is created.[9] The imminence of movement and displacement of specific and identified contents in the text is supposed to be one of the important conditions for the evolution of artistic situation by the standards of the presentation of acquired form to the external space. It would be rather necessary to justify the organisation of content of enriched form in universal and idealised conditions. There

9. *Dhvani* is intentionally situated on regular and complimentary models of variation within the circumstance of rationalisation, therefore, each of the categories has to be invented and intercepted just at the point of interception at which emotive experience and linguistic universalisation would cut each other. For further description on the subject, see Abhinavagupta:

समस्तगुणसम्पदः सममलङ्क्रियाणां गणै-
भर्वन्ति यदि भूषणं तव तथापि नो शोभसे।
शिवं हृदयवल्लभं यदि यथा तथा रञ्जये
स्तदेव ननुवाणि! ते भवति सर्वलोकोत्तरम्॥ – 2.5

can be at least two ways to bring about an interpretation of the situation. In the first place, we can understand that the process of finding out the exact predecessor and realistic successor to the completely realisable event becomes homogeneously perceptible and for this reason when external events evoke the content, the rationality of the whole event becomes thoroughly explicit. Ānandavardhana's consideration of native conjunction and co-native conjunction has a merit in itself because of the fact that external determinants of artistry are relatively weaker in embodying the exact value events. Therefore a necessity of concentrated and consolidated injunction is always felt and the conceptualisation of creating series of injunction for the revival of multiple authorities of artistic formation would certainly be an addition to the growth of absolute in the event. The worth of comprehending an adequate amount of refinement finally disposes every constructive situation through repeated succession of modification and changes or there might be an interdependant and interactive assimilation of the resultant value of each of such idealised form. Towards the end of the process/event we can get a sequence of multiple universals. In this situation, the function of artistry is to constantly activate the concentration of enrichment motif in suggesting the realisation of models with greater comprehensibility. For this reason the intention of an action on the part of *bhāva* is to make the change of enriched contents in both to be specific to the formal absolute that has emerged.

IV

The comprehension of *bhāva*, *vibhāva*, *anubhāva*, *sthāyībhāva* and others as specific and ideal instances of categorical construction introduces a method of creation of a large number of figural devices which can be introduced, employed and utilised for the sake of enhancement of the concentrated function inherent upon the situation at any point of time.[10] Ānandavardhana's *Dhvanyāloka* generally admits the direct formalisation through certain necessary changes in the scheme of presentation. He would say, for example:

व्यङ्ग्यस्य यत्राप्राधान्यं वाच्यमात्रानुयायिनः।
समासोक्त्यादयस्तत्र वाच्यालङ्कृतयः स्फुटाः।।

व्यङ्गस्य प्रतिभामात्रे वाच्यार्थानुगमेऽपि वा।
न ध्वनिर्यत्र वा तस्य प्राधान्यं न प्रतीयते।।

तत्परावेव शब्दार्थौ यत्र व्यङ्ग्यं प्रति स्थितौ।
ध्वने स एव विषयो मन्तव्याः सङ्करोज्झितः।। – 1.13

vyaṅgyasya yatrāprādhānyaṁ vācyamātrānuyāyinaḥ।
samāsoktyādayastatra vācyālaṅkṛtayaḥ sphuṭāḥ।।

vyaṅgasya pratibhāmātre vācyārthānugame 'pi vā।
na dhvaniryatra vā tasya prādhānyaṁ na pratiyate।।

tatparaveva śabdārtho yatra vyaṅgayaṁ prati sthitau।
dhvane sa eva viṣayo mantavyāḥ saṁkarojjhitaḥ।।

Ānandavardhana would like to substantiate the fact that the sequence of presentation of *śabda* and corresponding *bhāva* should be such that the consequential value of evolution from primary insignificance to secondary significance must be approached as a distinct situation and therefore the generative parts of the words in the idealised situation would yield an effective artistic situation. Looking at this, it can be immediately

10. Every figure of speech according to Ānandavardhana is a conscious projection of the intensity of rationalisation and each, therefore, has a substance in strengthening the totality and wholeness of artistic formation. For further description on the, subject, see Ānandavardhana:

ध्वन्यात्मभूते शृङ्गारे समीक्ष्य विनेवेशितः।
रूपकादिरलङ्कारवर्ग एति यथार्थताम्।। – 2.17

concluded that emergence of absolute artistic figures and the content could be made when and only when there is the exclusive formation of modifiable variants with a definite value configuration.

The actual creation of full-length body of the text would invariably compare two ideational forms of composition and first of which is to be related to concentration of differential transformation achieved on account of composite evolution therefore *bhāva* along with *sthāyībhāva* and *anubhāva* will enhance the speed of accumulation of the specific contents, and, on that account, it will have an opportunity to accelerate the formal modification. The second part of the situation, which is expected to bring about external correlatives together in such a way that effective and thoroughgoing reception of medium and content, involved in the upgradation and indexing of linguistic and emotive categories can be realised immediately.

The facts are observed to situate applicatory relevance through the artistic function proposed in John Donne's "Resurrection":

Sleep, Sleep old sun, thou canst not have repast
As yet, the wound thou took'st on Friday last;
Sleep then, and rest; the world may bear thy stay.
A better Sun rose before thee today,
Who, not content to enlighten all that dwell
On the earths face, as thou, enlightened hell,
And made the dark fires languish in that vale,
As, at thy presence here, our fires grow pale. — 1-8

In these verses we can understand that the progressive development of inquisition foresees and anticipates a concentration of knowledge, therefore, the inquisiton (the material form of existence) is fully embodied and internalised in the authority of an exceptional knowledge, that is, the sun.

The substantial part of comprehension grows out of an extensive process of evolution in which the strength of word (*sleep, sleep old sun*) and strength of meaning (*sun and better sun*) both are necessarily compounded giving rise to an aggregate multiple transformation so as to achieve the highest manner of artistic expression (*as, at thy presents here, our fires grow pale*). It is obviously a consequence of an interpretative form that derives from the magnification of an ordinary, primary inquisition into the highest stage of truthful introspection, yet both the stages present a common ground for exchange and comprehension. On that account, the experience is being invented (*sleep, sleep old sun*) and reinvented (*sleep then and rest*) and gradually the intermediate forms become evidently constructive for a revival at any instance; for example, the poet accepts the crises in experience by prefixing and interposing all the inversions and therefore he says: "*Thou can'st not have repast/As yet the wound thou took'st on Friday last/Sleep then and rest; the world may bear thy stay*". The basic property of the verses is to interact by identifying the significance as immediately as it has been introduced into the index and chronology or the experiential performance. By this standard, the configuration of the words "sleep old sun" would form an event that has continuously received the highest state of transformation inasmuch as all the preceding words (sleep, as yet, the wound, rest, the world, thy stay, better) bring about unification for the sake of an absolute form that culminates into the absolute and unquestionably most resolute form of experience in the sun and the situation of *dhvani* is thoroughly explicated. There might be the possibility to suggest, in the next place, that all the words in the verses opt and propose an index of performance for them inasmuch as sleep (in sleep sleep old sun) would stand for a deviation forming synthesis of ideological crisis in being not able to purify and perfect to this extent in the lifetime. Similarly, wound (wound then took'st on Friday last) will have multiple conjunction in ascribing an optimum invention for the sake of infinity or loss that generates affection for affective pleasures. On the whole, the verses display the strength for an assertive interpretation and examination for the theoretical form which we have developed, and, on that account, it would be really better to state that continuity of resolution from *śabda* to *vākya* on the one hand, and from *bhāva* to *anubhāva* on the other, would exactly define the exceptional merit created by inclusive modification throughout and consistently. *Śabda* is a primary occasion that inaugurates the critical experience, the poet is having (sleep) while the prolongation of *śabda* is stylistically absorbed in the tenure of the whole *vākya* (sleep, sleep old sun thou canst have repast). While, at the same time, inventory is posited through constant modification proposed by *bhāva* (*karuṇa* expressive through *glāni, lajjā* and *dainya*). A better sun rose before thee today/ Who, not content to enlighten all that dwell/On the earth's face, as thou, enlightened hell. The extraordinary correspondence generated by the *śabda* for an inquisition of an exact value in *bhāva* is one of the fine instances of poetic comprehension and composition that would be seen and understood.

Dhvani, for that matter, must be exactly understood to be as the creation of the highest absolute, truthful and total value of the contents, medium, form and the whole event. The creation of value, also, at the same time, determines and fixes up the significant form of artistic situation that is going to emerge as a consequence of the continuity of evolution, transformation and transmutation of *śabda* into *bhāva*, *bhāva* into *pada* and *pada* into *bhāva* and that is unquestionably the greatest strength that the artistry could be having.[11]

11. The manner of imitation and the quality of transformation, both appear to be extraordinarily enriched inasmuch as the enrichment of the categories leads to the finality and totality. For further description on the subject, see Rājaśekhara:

यास्तर्ककर्कशानर्थान्सूक्तिष्वाद्रियते कविः।
सूर्याश्च इवेन्दौ ते काञ्चिदर्चन्ति कान्ताम।। – 8

V

Structuralist poetics deals with a situation in which the units of language, like the words, letters, syllables expressively obtain a truthful change for themselves in such a way that both, the language and meaning, enter into a framework of combination, correspondence, exposition and, to an extent, cognition.[12] The extent of generation of meaning presupposes an idealistic form of functionality to be achieved in the general set-up of phonetic, semantic, semiotic, morphological and syntactical circumstances of expression and the synthesis achieved in such a way or manner produces the absolute of value in the form of an index.

The strength so obtained makes out an evidence of distinction between the units of language proposed and obtained through a simultaneity of generation while the larger effects are excluded only to expand the process of transformation of linguistic and emotive events. It must be clear as to how and why word, letter, syllable and sentence on the one hand, enter into a combinatory framework with corresponding experience in an imagination, thought and the like. In this act of correspondence, transformation is intended and, for this reason, the association of a unit of experience with that of language would bring about a creation of evolution as a fundamental principle of change in the artistic event. There

---

12. In the structuralist poetics, cognitive variants of the categories undergo multiple transformation hence entail totality in the artistry. The idea of langue and parole as developed by Saussure must be understood in terms of the progression of the content for the sake of radical modification in which every organisation is due to langue and every change for that matter just because of the activity of parol. It would also uphold the Western metaphysics purporting a distinction between matter and form, body and soul, actuality and potentiality. For further description on the subject, see Culler.

is a primary basis in presuming that the units of language like words and syllables invent a construction in which a determination and fixation of the worth of generative language and experience take place and afterwards an approval for the reinvention of the configural form is made and suitability of such a process is enhanced just on account of the fact that cohesion, symmetry, harmony and explicit formation of conjugal form is almost entirely evident. In other words, we can say that structuralist situation facilitates the transformation of object into event by incorporating standardisation of value through unique and exceptional configuration given to the contents of language and constructs of the meaning. Every normative and procedural advancement in setting up a committed, authentic and firm configuration upgrades the manner of synthesis through revival of more concentrated, compact and consolidated terms in the categories. For this reason, language and experience proposed to distinguish categorical forms through which the whole procedure of evolution is expected to be initiated and obtained. At any point of time, we can understand that linguistic contents like letters, syllables, words, sentences and paragraphs and experiential models like experience, imagination and thought would firmly and succinctly conjoin to enhance suitability for themselves so as to enter into an act of resolution and exactly at that the function of evolution of language into meaning is rendered. The accomplishment of the process generating a formalised and constructive form of meaning apparatus and a good deal of presupposition conceived in concrete linguistic constructs create two important events in the growth of structuralist poetics. Inevitably, the large explications are also conceived, of which the linguistics experiencial formation in myth appears to be very important. Now, to understand the methodology of the formal functioning of structuralist poetics, we will have to take into consideration the concentrated form evident in all the units of language and all the units of experience.

Words constitute the core of generative situation in the artistic set-up and for that matter word could be described to be as a form of inception in which the possibility of association is supposed to be the maximum besides association. It also tends to interpolate a scale of insertion for subtractive and multiplicatory evidence and inference derived from the immediately cognised event holding a score of value for them.[13] In structuralist tradition, the conception of words falls upon the suppositional and post-suppositional attitudes evoked by a word, and, in this context, it would be better to make mention of the fact that immediate application and extensive conjunction suggested by contextulised orientation would be maximum when and only when the word is conceived as a form capable of inducting identity and assertion as evidences of value creation. In fact, when a form is substantiated through primary function, for example, it can be made to obtain the elementary level value, and, in that case, it will only conform to concentration of formal synthesis. In any event, such a form will invent an exact situation for itself through a significant deviation developed from within the various interrelations achieved as a part of expression. The qualitative manner in which word is expressed approves its constitutional feature in that every upward movement in a word implicates an evidence of variation brought about by letter and the syllable. In structuralist tradition, however, the subsistence of the primary form is supposed to be generally and always forming correlative to the immediate conjunction, therefore, production of value at the behest of primary notation would yield a possibility of interpreting the equivalence through similar notation achieved in the secondary

---

13. Multiplication is essentially a virtue in that it enhances the prospects of expansion. This adds all the enriched contents to the artistic formation. For further description on the subject, see Jakobson.

situation. Thus, absolute content function and nearly complete content change could be approved on account of such displacements observed in word position. The actual conception of word in structuralist manner of thinking must be considered to be as a part of a causation proposed for the sake of the advancement of marginal units lying almost in the capacity of supplementary situations. The necessity of such a presentation depends on how the direction of movement of letter or syllable is contained within the aspects of reason and stability. To this extent, one has to say that the elementary part of word, although invented by external deterministic form for the sake of cohesion, could desolve itself into unequal categories. There can be certain ways to establish the function of determinate sequence form within the word by a very extensive and rich association that is cohesively devised for the sake of the significance of interpretation. In a word, the extension of synthesis is causative to the extent that it can prolong and extend the inter-functional unit, for example, a letter could be substantially intended to exceed the term of inception just by maintaining the upward act of association. Now question must be asked as to how and why the urgency of association is natural, while, on the other hand, the act of association so thoroughly valuised that, except under strong force of context, there cannot be an act of association! It can be stated with conviction that content within the word is always activated in relation to appropriate time sequence in which the form of association is inevitably manifest, and when the conjugations are absolute marks of context are indexed and listed preferentially. In the early stages, the manner of expansion of a word is both by allowing its extension in linear and cyclical direction, and, for the same reason, the manner of extension doesn't clearly express itself through correlation, rather it is substantiated more precisely in inversion. The effect that obviously comes could be understood in the manner of the following arrangement in which the possibility of exclusion and inclusion are intended:

$$A = A(a) + B(b) + C(c) + D(d) \ldots\ldots n$$

If *A* is accepted and understood in the form of a totality that is presupposed on account of its advancement by opening both the visual and non-visual sequence of embodiment. For this reason, aggregate word will be characteristically be disposed through real aggregate in supplementary contents expressed in terms of *A* and its variant *a*. The conformity to the situation amounts to an important event of the growth of concept in structuralist situation. Even otherwise, in an artistic situation, the poetical rendering is clearly embodied in the juxtaposition of a word with its variants either in the form of letter or syllable, although, it is a different thing that the situation sometimes is noticeable and sometimes it is not. In any event, the modality of precision would remain an authoritative function to generate and determine the worth of the contents. For Saussure, the question of acceptance of word as a model of association with the preceding and succeeding visual and non-visual forms would ultimately be a question of inducting radical and empirical attitudes, and for that matter, association eventually becomes a process of reinvention in which both the empirical part and the figurative part have the same intensity of assertion. In fact, the empirical side retains its hold on content of expression. This could prove the point that evolution of content is immediately conceived in notional word that is open for experiential notation by the virtue of its ability to invest in accordance with the force of the medium and the context. In the structuralist tradition the following five principle characteristics of a word could be made mention of: (1) Additive, (2) Multiplicative, (3) Associative, (4) Subtractive, (5) Divisive; and in accordance with the condition generated in each of these characteristics we have the creation of meaning in each of the above situations. Now, we will proceed to examine in somewhat great detail the analytical part that inheres within each of the above situations.

In the structuralist manner of conceptualisation, words would come up for an expression of the total meaning strength developed and gathered by the inner form and outward functionality.[14] This particular situation is brought about when the context is making its movements and some logical displacements acquire motivated interrelationship, and, for that matter, the advancement towards meaning is marked by a process of invention of a group of interrelated objects. This would mean that every cohesive word has an equal opportunity of generating simultaneous effect of conjunction provided the movement of context along the medium is assured. Saussure agrees to the situation and states the basic effect of the problem in what he would like to call signification:

> I propose to retain the word sign [signe] to designate the whole and to replace concept and sound-image respectively by signified [signifié] and signifier [significant]; the last two terms have the advantage of indicting the opposition that separates them from each other and from the whole of which they are parts. — 67

Saussure insists on the presentation of a constancy to restore continuity in the matter of evolution of word into its significant form with a distinct associative function. This is, therefore, a basic condition that could form a method of suggesting that movements of primary words, along with phonetic and morphological forms, obviously adopt a distinction in synthesising the last term of expression. The growth of word

14. The idea of meaning in accordance with the structuralist proposition would evidently be the manner in which selection of enriched categories is made. This would lead to the transformation through which finally a standardised pattern will make its appearance. For further description on the subject, see Chomsky.

as a substantial standard of expression would make us believe that the capacity to carry out substitution and certain other readjustments by implicating every forthcoming content with noteworthy correlations, for example, the word *A* is generally suited to come at the beginning to mark a subdivision derived from itself in the manner of *a* and *b* so as to identify the progression of a variation. Artistically the projection of the word at the beginning will constitute two distinct yet heterogeneous devisions of itself in such a way that every division is also an aggregate of the compound function generated simultaneously from within the participating models. In fact, it would be better to say that the morphological inquisition within a word would only correspond to the relative forms explicitly intended in semiotic and semantic function, therefore, we can at least investigate the authority of form in the following arrangement of the variable:

$$\sum = \frac{\frac{a}{a(a)}}{a(a \times a)} + \frac{\frac{b}{b(b)}}{b(b \times b)} + \frac{\frac{c}{c(c)}}{c(c \times c)} + \ldots \ldots \ldots . n$$

The intensity of aggregate content that is Σ would follow the possible extent of variation obtained in *a*, *b*, *c* as determinate variables and consequences. For this reason, the intention of association appears first hand as a beginning of a division within a division so as to achieve the absolute and discard the inconsequential aggregate of presentation. In fact, there would be a continuity of progression till the time relevant variables of the words, letters, syllables are determined and achieved. The necessity of conjugating the principality of assertive content is actually injuncted through multiple dispersions acting upon a situation. What actually happens is that the first term of committed correspondence of actual content to prospective content is invented through both the external and internal spatial models, and for this reason, term of progress in relation to any backward or advancing full length content will form an exact continuity of growth.[15] It is because of the foregoing principles that the suitability of arrangement follows the principle of convergence through multiple denotations. The manner of interpretation assumes a rather formal feature in associating the growth of any content as a part of the forthcoming generation of multiple variants. In *Abhijñānaśākuntalam* of Kālidāsa, for example, there would be an apportunity to find out exact suitability of the principle of expansion developed by the structuralists:

मुक्तेषु रश्मिषु निरायतपूर्वकाया।
निष्कम्पचामरशिखा निभृतोर्ध्वकर्णाः।।

आत्मोध्दतैरपि रजोभिरलङ्घनीया।
धावन्त्यभी मृगजवाक्षमयेव रथ्याः।। – 1.8

muktesu raśmisu nirāyatapūrvakāyā ।
niṣkampacāmaraśikhā nibhṛtordhvakarṇāḥ ।।

ātmodhdatairapi rajobhiralaṅghanīyā ।
dhāvantyabhī mṛgajavākṣamayeva rathyāḥ ।।

In these verses the situation of the content is precisely expository while the manner of association is distinctly empirical, therefore, the poet makes the charioteer to explicate the evidences of appearance and disappearance of deer and the method of situating the order of experience is quite remarkable. In the first place, the concurrence of assimilation is forthrightly expressed in "मुक्तेषु रश्मिषु निरायतपूर्वकाया", suggesting thereby that the deer has finally disappeared. The progress of the content has assumed the manner of addition inasmuch

15. Addition and subtraction of the content could also add to the realisation of organic forms. For further description on the subject, see Saussure.

as the objects of experience are supposed to be invented in a cyclical progression, and, consequently, because of the same, the poet says — "निष्कम्पचामरशिखा" thus generating a value that would confer the status of an absolute sign function inasmuch as it would restore the indivisible nature to its formal sanctity. Similarly, the evidence of association is almost generative, for example, the poet says: "आत्मोध्दतैरपि रजोभिरलङ्घनीया धावन्त्यमी मृगजवाक्षमयेव रथ्या:।" Here the method of interpretation follows the exact determination of semantic and semiotic configuration inasmuch as the movement of the deer and the movement of the chariot have raised dust so much so that each is invisible to each and on that account we could state that both the object and subject are formally rendered more signification to their own accounts, hence it comes as an addition to the figurative part of semiotic and semantic regeneration.

The significance of proportion suggested by the absolute form in the above verse, could be seen to be having distinct faces of correlation for that matter the inversion suggested in "मुक्तेषु" is having the optimum concentration in "निष्कम्पचामरशिखा" and "निभृतोर्ध्वकर्णा". The condition of inquisition supports the independent assortment of semantic, semiotic and morphological objects, therefore, the structuralist interpretation is obviously generated.

The quality of comprehension, rooted in methodically accurate denotative form, is carried on and suggested by the virtue of an extension of emplied variants, therefore, the possibility of bringing together the categories and content, like words and syllables, would prove to be a primary expression given to the aspect of multiplication.[16] By

16. Structuralism is quite precisely the manner of thinking in which categories like thought, language, etc. undergo functional appropriation and on that account value comes to be added to each of these categories. In the Saussurian system every unit of language is open for the sake of functionality →

multiplication of the categories in the structuralist tradition, one would obviously mean the generation of value in accordance with the extraction of variants within variants, and, for that matter, the following proposition would hold good for the fact of significance stated herein:

$$A\,(a) = a+b+c\,\ldots\ldots\,n$$

This could prove to be rather an expressive manner of presentation held functionality responsible for the expansion of a linguistic/emotive situation. This could be obviously an achievement of preferential function and concentrated function in the manner in which word is supposed to be obtained and projected simultaneously as a marker of prospective correlation beyond the conventional and orthodox situation. It follows from this that implicative situations obtained in a word, disassociate both the letter and syllable, and on the other hand, revive a prospect of regeneration through certain practices. It could be seen that these two are independent segments through which the progress of a category in the form of a whole is assured. In the first place, there is a continuity of counter as well as relative formation of the value, therefore, the variant that holds actually realised content is opened for the sake of the next or forthcoming inception. In that way any variable is expected to be having two complimentary models of representation, Saussure observes:

> Where distincition should be made according to the following illustration, between (1) the axis of simultaneities (*AB*), which stands for the relations of coexisting things and from which the intervention of time is excluded; and (2) the axis of successions (*CD*), on which only one thing can be considered at a time but upon which are located all the things on the first axis together with their changes. — 80

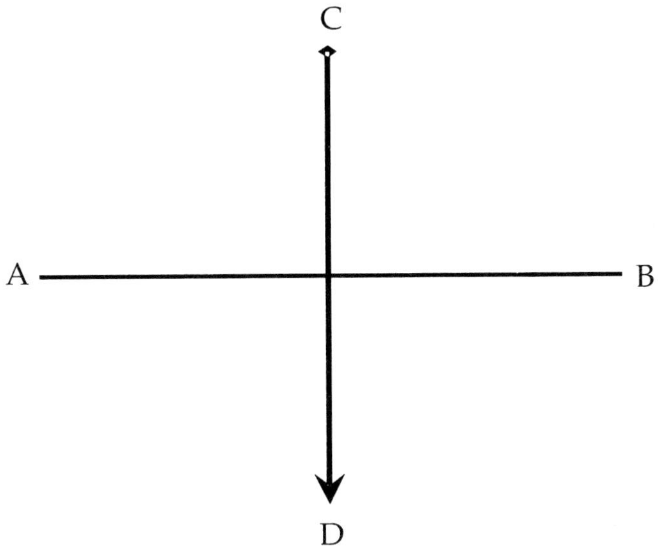

We can notice and understand that the real variables of language proceed to have the changes in the same way, there might also be a situation in which both the structure and function are supposed to be stationary and stagnant. While this situation is observed, the position and authenticity of word as word and meaning as meaning would be generally affected. For example, while we understand the evolution of modern "Father" from either Sanskrit "पितृ" (*pitr̥*) or Latin "Patri", it becomes quite easy to understand that the effect of time on language is consequential through the important replacement it makes with regard to both the spelling and pronunciation. Similarly, the finally evolved word "Father" is supposed to be having constancy for a certain period of time, making the contention fix that the process of change and the period of stability correspond to each other and therefore, be it simultaneous (not fit for the changes) or succession (suitable to the changes). The act of correspondence shall continue to uphold the merit of assertion. In the structuralist tradition, this idea becomes very important inasmuch as it becomes suggestive of the fact that meaning originates from the preceding situation and will continue to hold fast to the succeeding form that is going to emerge. In effect modality could now be built to find out the consistency of the rationalised forms expressed in Saussurian terms:

$$A^a = A = B^b$$

In this arrangement, we can understand that the manner of generation of *A* is born out of the primodial existence of its ealier variations in originary *a* and it is futher expanded by a correlative intended in succession. On the other hand, the point is thoroughly established that incidental and successive forms need to harmonise the process of meaning formation inasmuch as the act of rationality and the significance of truth have immediately become worthy and noticeable. The extent of argument presented in the foregoing comments would amount to stating the fact that the invention of a new form is subjected to pure and optimum synthesis brought about by exact and concentrated variants in the previous stages of its evolution. For example, look at the following situation in Ādiparva of *Mahābhārata*:

त्वदर्थमागता, भद्रे, क्षत्रियाः, प्रथिता भुवि।
विध्यते य इदं लक्ष्यं, वरयेथाः, शुभेऽद्यतम्।। – 31

tvadarthamāgatā, bhadre, kṣatriyāḥ, prathitā bhuvi ।
vidhyate ya idaṁ lakṣyaṁ, varayethāḥ, śubhe 'dyatam ।।

In this passage the act of synthesis for that matter, the creation of meaning (piercing the eye of the moving fish is based on the evidence of direct multiplication of the terms, therefore, the cause (लक्ष्यं वरयेथाः) proposes a formative inscription in the manner of the people who have assembled from all across of the world (क्षत्रियाः, प्रथिता भुवि). While the conditions to this effect are manifested in the succession, the whole intention is outlined through (वरयेथाः शुभेऽद्यतम्) (getting married to the best). Now looking at each of the words, we could immediately conclude that there is a constituted dispensation that has been assigned to the words, therefore, every preceding word is equivalent to every succeeding word, hence — त्वदर्थमागता भद्रे, क्षत्रियाः प्रथिता, इदं लक्ष्यं would ultimately lead to शुभेऽद्य and we could produce the following arrangement for the situation:

$$\Sigma = a \times b \ldots\ldots n$$

The actual circumstance of the production of the content via multiplication is basically an effect that is based on a prominent revival of an exact linguistic form. For example, introduction of a word at any point of time would subverse the natural order of intensity of configuration, and, therefore, Saussure insists on the fact that there has to be a division between the independent yet interrelated order of presentation of a word.[17] In this context, it will be possible to state that continuity and discontinuity mounted on selected form of a word shall be exactly indicating an actual strength. For this reason, the intersection of word *a* with word *b* would ultimately produce a meaning that will have the best term for regeneration. There can be at least two different ways to look at the whole problem, and, in the first place, the act of multiplication does not exclude the other varieties of combination and association. Generally, the introduction of a word in a sentence extends the probability of correlation; accordingly it will lead to the creation of the multiples of conjunction in such a way that both the vertical

→ and thus every category must acquire value, fit and appropriate for itself. For further description on the subject, see Culler.

17. Functionality of categories is a circumstance of immediate reality that is conceived in pragmatic value to be added to the artistic formation. In the similar context an ideal word would be one that is capable of invocating significant patterns of value by relying on the three stage configuration, that is signifier, sign and signified. For further description on the subject, see Barthes.

and horizontal orders are preferentially and realistically elevated. Similarly, if *a* is the word intending a situation in the sentence *z* then the progress of such a form would include vertical multiples as well as horizontal parts of the attributes and variables, consequently *A* will be represented as:

$$\begin{array}{|c|}\hline A\\ a\\ b\\ c\\ d\\ \hline\end{array}$$

Similarly, the horizontal function would include a series of associative function characterised as:

$$\boxed{B^{abcd}}$$

This explains the basic nature of value formation in multiplicative orientation of the hightened linguistic/emotive forms.

In the structuralist tradition, the idea of multiplication of the contents would mean the primary ability of the models, contents and category (words, letters, syllables, and the sentence) to generate an exact equivalent for themselves. For that matter, models and categories enter into an inter-generative system, in which every category is supposed to bring about a larger variant of itself in which the exponential function puts the creation of value, growth of function and generation of a form world identically be the parts of the primary situation that would sustain the basic ideal of expansion, and accordingly, the first primary model will out of necessity introduce variants within itself by explicating formally assorted conjunction, and for this reason, the formation of a concentric circle will intend the growth of the categories and would be not a fact outside the formal part of the structure. In fact, the emergence of the method of equal reciprocation by proceeding and succeeding terms of reciprocation, the facility to induct larger variants would at once be absolute and perfect. Look at the following figure for an example:

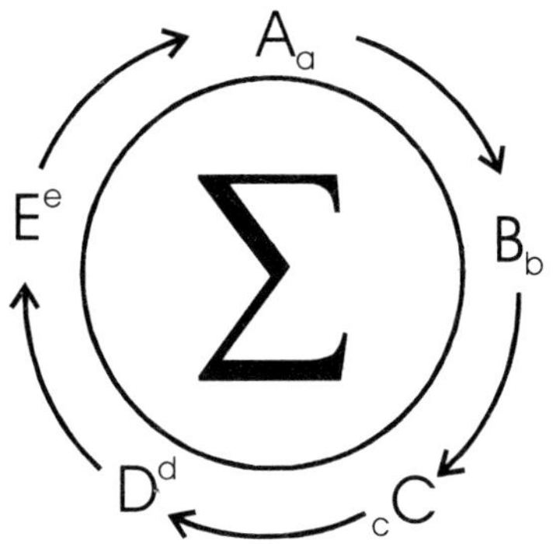

In this illustration we can understand that the function of a value is equal to the structure of the originary form and for that matter every event of expansion will also be the time of native perpetuation. Roman Jakobson would suggest that there must be a situationary function between two formulative parts of the same contents:

> What is the empirical linguistic criterion of the poetic function? In particular, what is the indispensable feature inherent in any piece of poetry? To answer this question we must recall the two basic modes of arrangement used in verbal behaviour, selection and combination. . . . The poetic function projects the principle of equivalence from the axis of selection into the axis of combination. — 39

The manner of contention presents certain uniqueness about the fact of multiplication. The advancement of correlation amongst the words is certainly a property that leads to the inclusion of a word into the word so as to suggest a typical situation in which a value interacts itself and forms a multiple of equivalences. For that matter, the idea of correspondence would hold good inasmuch as every act of passing on of certain codes to the next competent unit would be a method of finding out how and why the existence of a correlation in one particular situation determines the existence somewhat similar code in the other situation.[18] Jakobson insists on the fact that the term of progress of a word in a congenial situation depends on the extent of idealised intensity created in two successive parts of the same event. Accordingly, if *A*, *B* and *C* are having a manner of association then the third will automatically be brought to an extent of refinement in such a way that there would be the revival of strength in both the previous contents and naturally the third instance would generate the maximum possibility of transforming the entire range of contents. In fact, Jakobson suggests not only the transfer but reworking of both the medium and the content so much so that a thoroughgoing index is developed to situate the maximum possibility of suggestivity. The nature of extension formed within the words invariably determines under what context and because of what manner will the words have the enlargement of situated content against the extended contents. Nevertheless, the position of the letters within the words and syllables within the words devise a continuity of methodically rich proposition to continue the process of multiplication. As an event multiplication of content with content within a word and outside a word would be based on reliability and suitability of external situations, otherwise the process and the effect both are in a way halted. For example, look at the following situation in Sabhāparva of the *Mahābhārata*:

ततः समुत्थाय स राजपुत्रः,
श्रुत्वा भ्रातः शासनं रक्त-दृष्टिः।
प्रविश्य-तद वे म महारथानां,

18. The constitution of sign is a matter of addition of the enriched contents to the situation and it is of necessity that every realistic content should convert itself to the process of enrichment inasmuch as it could develop into a sign. For further description on the subject, see Culler.

इत्यब्रवीद् द्रौपदीं राज-पुत्रीम् ॥"

एह्येहि पांचालि, जितासि कृष्णे,
दुर्योधनं प य विमुक्त-लज्जा,
करुन भजस्वायत्-पध्म-नेत्रे
धर्मेण लब्धासिसभां परैहि ॥ – 100, 101

tataḥ samutthāya sa rājaputraḥ,
śrutvā bhrātaḥ śāsanaṁ rakta-dr̥ṣṭiḥ ।

praviśya-tada ve ma mahārathānāṁ,
ityabravīd draupadīṁ rāja-putrīm ॥

ehyehi pāñcāli, jitāsi kr̥ṣṇe,
duryodhanaṁ pa ya vimukta-lajjā ।

karuna bhajasvāyat-padhma-netre
dharmeṇa labdhāsisabhāṁ paraihi ॥

In these verses, the function of language is to create an individualised model of transformation in such a way that the position of a word and situation of the meaning is absolutely functionalised and the whole idea is conceived through the logic of displacement and substitution ultimately leading to the production of the effect of multiplication. In other words, we can say that every word in the given verse, is in a position to create a universal value for itself and the content of value, is precisely so inverted that it leads to the creation of generative equivalence, hence the function of multiplication is explained. Now Duḥśāsana appears on the stage and commands Draupadī, an inversion of injunction by modifying herself into someone who nearly looks like a servant or a slave. The command of Duḥśāsana enacts a series of inquisition and therefore each inquisition is recreated into an expanding unit and therefore he could say: "ऐह्येहि पांचालि". Now the manner of producing a unit of expansion is supposedly so expressive that it immediately turns into its equivalent value and therefore we have "धर्मेण लब्धासिसभां परैहि". The scale and immensity of modification of the units of language are so rich and high that the scale of meaning that is produced invents a significant manner of multiplication. While we understand the structuralist implication in the verses of the *Mahābhārata,* the attention is sometime invited to discover a pattern through which an evolutionary pattern is suggested. In the first place, we can make it a point that generative value is necessarily created out of the strength of injunction in the formative contents and with this particular intention the process of modification becomes very simple and highly enriched. In Jakobson's observation the idea of combination and selection are mooted to find out the length and extent of participation made by those units of the language, which are specifically meant to commit themselves to employ injunction. For that matter, morphological, syntactical, phonological forms appear to be more suited for this purpose.

The correspondence of value, with an intention to acquire a shape and form of exact meaning oriented configuration is one of the aspects that has attracted the attention of major structuralists, and, for that matter, compulsive or impulsive assortment of categories like word, sentence, and syllable, would obtain a concrete universal for their own sake. In approving the method of legitimate situation, one could think of the fact that the word is displaced and brought back by the explication of an empirical form that attends on it hence the immediacy and constancy of evolution is fixed and maintained. At two given generative units, the capacity of a word to enlarge the cognitive form would be the best option that would initiate the creation of a sequence of optimum creative strength for a word, and exactly at this stage, we could understand how association as a method of generation of value is important.

> A lexia is obviously a textual signifier; but at our job here is not to observe signifiers (our work is not stylistic) but

> meanings, . . . the lexia is an arbitrary product, it is simply a segment within which the distribution of meanings is observed. . . . The useful lexia is one where only one, two or three meanings take place, . . . By meaning we mean the cannotation of the lexia, the secondary meanings. — 173

Barthes, as above suggests that the function of a word is to create those models of vertical concept which are necessarily subjected to interfunctional changes in such a way that only the value of correlation is retained whereas the primary strength is relegated to the background. In other words, we can say that the extent of emergence of an object and its multiples or variants in the form of subject derives from the idea that signifiers are attatched to the roots through the implications that subsist between the realised and realisable parts of the significance. We can also understand that the function of word is only to appropriate and determine the sequence of fixed value. For this reason, the movement of a word in a progressive direction brings about certain value specific changes, and therefore, Barthes' conception may be said to, have held ground. Even otherwise, the necessity of introducing certain changes through the propulsion and inception of right word at the right time could be inducted into the appropriate textual environment only to facilitate the recovery of primary relation and primary association. The artistic environment brings about a method of inducting a structure of enrichment by implanting explicit scale of movement so that every construct shall have, at least, an equivalent correlative form for itself.[19] This is to say, in other words, that the realistic condition of the structure of language is guided and controlled by the union of one content with the

19. In an artistic formation the composition of meaning must be the mark of excellence. In structuralism, meaning is inadvertently the product of the process of evolution. What evolves therefore, is the structure. For further description on the subject, see Guillen.

other and the approval of the fact is generally found to be substantiated by the regression of received and carried on through the functional word. For example, if *A* and *B* are two imminent forms then association of *A* with *B* or *B* with *A* would depend on how the artistic situation appropriate to *A* is similar in content to that of *B* and for that matter the strength of correlation compounded to *A* will also move towards *B* inasmuch as both have a ground of similarity, and, for the same reason, number of contents joined upon *A* will be similar to that we have in *B*, and accordingly, we will have an association between *A* and *B*. Jakobson makes a point of significance when he says:

> The ADDRESSER sends a MESSAGE to the ADDRESSEE. To be operative, the message requires a CONTEXT referred to ('referent' in another, somewhat ambiguous, nomenclature), seizable by the addressee and either verbal or capable of being verbalised, a code fully, or at least partially, common to the addresses and addressee (or in other words, to the encoder and decoder of the message); and, finally, a CONTACT a physical channel and psychological connection between the addresser and the addressee, enabling both of them to enter and stay in communication. All these factors inalienably involved in verbal communication may be schematised as follows:
>
> CONTEXT
> MESSAGE
> *ADDRESSER*________________________________*ADDRESSEE*
> CONTACT
> CODE

Each of these six factors, determine a different function of language. Growth of the terms inherent in a situation is virtually manifest in how language is modified into the parts and in that way the parts become the intention and an aspect of the wholesome formation, and, for this reason, Jakobson suggests that there is an existence of an object and the subject as a part of mutual readjustment and conversion. And the event eventually leads to the creation of standardised meaning and formalised thoughts about the contents of the evolution. Communication of the content of language could be understood to be a simplified method or procedure to initiate the manner of change and for this reason in Jakobson's scheme the addresser is ultimately revived in the addressee. Meaning thereby that the value of *A* has been exactly added to the value of *A* and therefore, the strength of *A* is now equal to *A* and the additive contents that we could find in-between the models of enrichment are truthfully the carriers of the approved version of a resolution. Consequently, in the context, contact message and code we will have a procedural division of the growth of significance. It is possible to suggest the dichotomy of form and content by initiating and conducting an aggregate term of change. In each of the stages of enrichment there is a confirmation of the actual strength and the realistic value, therefore, contact would carry double the value of the addresser hence, the same component of value would be further redoubled in the context and with the achievement of the last term, that is, addressee, the process is nearly complete.[20] In the event in which we put forth two major terms in relation to these respective values, we could only confirm if the appropriateness of generated value is rightly placed in the content or not. If the situation is otherwise, then immediately we could understand that there is a variation in the length and intensity of the enrichment, and, for the same reason, the commitment of object towards the event is approved.

---

20. Organic process is conspicuous in the method of artistic evolution approached in the structuralist poetics. The terms of organicity are realised in sifting, expunging, combining and finally ordering the transformation. Linguistic contents and experiential models, both are routed through the adequacy of context, medium and content. Hence, there is the appropriateness of the circumstance. For further description on the subject, see Genette.

The consequence of association is felt and understood to be precisely more in creation of an artistic situation. Barthes, for example, would like to examine the possibility of having an idealised, and, for that matter, deterministic version of native formation like, for example, the language of ordinary and actual conversation and the language that the poet writes and that which is once again based on investigating mythological properties out of a given situation. Then ultimately the ethical essence would upgrade the gradual structuring and ordering of the whole material into a significant form. In the following observation of Barthes, the situation is approved as having been built around the similar sets of contradiction and apposition:

> The ecrivain fulfils a function, the ecrivant an activity, that much we learn from grammar, which rightly opposes the substantive of the one to the (transitive) verb of the other. Not that the ecrivain is a pure essence: he acts, but his action is immanent to its object, it is exercised, paradoxically, on its own instrument: language; the ecrivain is someone who works on his language (even if inspired) and is functionally obsorbed into that work. The activity of the ecrivain involves two types of norm: technical ones (of composition, genre, writing) and artisanal ones (of work, patience, correcting, perfecting). The paradox is that, the raw material having become in some ways its own end, literature is basically a tautological activity . . . the ecrivain is one who absorbs the . . . the world radically into a how to write. And the miracle, if we can put it like that, is that all through the literary ages this narcissistic activity has not ceased to pose a question to the world. . . . — 66

According to Barthes, the act of transformation of writer into the object and object into the writer, or for that matter the codes into the fact or ideas into the index, is a process that is completed only when there is conformity to the value and structure, and, for this reason, it is necessary that the writer should explicate the structure of the object by intending a complete and thoroughgoing assessment of association between the correspondence of imminent structures. Writer could create the values in accordance with the intensity of the structure, and therefore, object could also show similar intensity and value. The association, will, however, depend on the way in which the unit of structure would enter into a series of changes into the corresponding part. The product therefore would be the specific significance of the meaning that is going to be created. In the entire structuralist discourse, association is purely a necessity of semantic order obviating and fixing the pattern of acceptance and condition of changing primary terms into secondary intention, and, for that matter, the inclusion of functional units becomes more or less the principal instruments for revival of a meaningful condition. In Barthes viewpoint, the understanding is actually explained with the help of the discovery of the foundation of the structure of meaning that is hidden almost entirely in the idea of object and subject expressed through the writer and the object of writing, or for that matter author and the work. Actual completion of the process of semantic significance, upholds the merit of the act of association, therefore, in the following verses of Ayodhyā Kāṇḍa of the *Rāmāyaṇa* the aggregate of the situation is significantly complete:

मम वृद्धस्य कैकेयि गतांतस्य तपस्विनम्।
दीनं लालप्यमानस्य कारुण्यं कर्तुमर्हसि।।

पृथिव्यां सागरतायां यत्किंचिदधिगम्यते।
तत्सर्वं तव दास्यामि मा च त्वं मृत्युमाविश।।

अंजलिं कुर्मि कैकेयि पादौ चापि स्पृशामि ते।
शरणं भव रामस्य माऽधर्मो मामिह स्पृशेत्।। – 34, 35, 36

mama vṛddhasya kaikeyi gatāṁtasya tapasvinam ।
dīnaṁ lālapyamānasya kāruṇyaṁ kartumarhasi ।।

pṛthivyāṁ sāgaratāyāṁ yatkiñcidadhi gamyate ।
tatsarvaṁ tava dāsyāmi mā ca tvaṁ mṛtyumāviśa ॥

añjaliṁ kurmi kaikeyi pādau cāpi spṛśāmi te ।
śaraṇaṁ bhava rāmasya ma 'dharmo māmiha spṛśet ॥

In these verses the model and sequence of contents have been suitably established and accomplished. For this reason the opening of the verses is marked by the conjunction and flexibility, therefore, the generative appropriateness in मम वृद्धस्य with an addition of apostrophised noun, we have the making of signification in कारुण्यं कर्तुमर्हसि. Similarly, the length of extension generated to a particular lexus is built around the fact that the positive inclination and negative orientation will ultimately reduce the content, yet, however the accidental emergence of a modifier converts the entire sequence into circumstantially idealised condition. On the other hand, the term of resolution accepts the position of signifiers, hence, Daśaratha would say: "शरणं भव रामस्य माऽधर्मो मामिह स्पृशेत". It could be understood that the function adopted in the verses could commute the position of signifiers (कैकेयि, राम) and hence appropriate the whole proposition in the transmutation of addresser Daśaratha and addressee Kaikeyī. It is almost certain at this stage that the motif of semantic injunction (कारुण्यं कर्तुमर्हसि) is to expand the extent of variation within and outside the signified, and, therefore, Daśaratha invents a critical function both in sign and object (दीनं, पृथिव्यां, सागरतायां, अंजलिं कुर्मि). The evidence of structuralist function is also manifest in unusual syntactic movement for the sake of modification adopted in the verses. Therefore, lengthening of such words as — पृथिव्यां, सागरतायां, अंजलिं कुर्मि, माऽधर्मो मामिह स्पृशेत, produce the effect of combination in those words which necessarily bear an identity to the mark of value. Now the whole formulation could be substantiated in the following manner:

वृद्धस्य	कारुण्यं	मृत्युमाविश	अंजलि कुर्मि	मामिह स्पृशेत
A	B	C	D	E
↓	↓	↓	↓	↓
कैकेयि	मा च त्वं	कैकेयि	ते भव	रामस्य
A	B	C	D	E

In these sets of utterances the extent of significance and intensity of communication could be realised by promoting the lexus to advance the relative signified by inventing the native form in each. Thus, in these verses the propriety of communication is so well adjusted that syntactical function immediately corresponds to significatory exposition, and, therefore sequential absolutes are chronologically invented inasmuch as the first absolute in कैकेयि corresponds to reversible universal in कारुण्यं कर्तुमर्हसि, and, therefore, there is a full-scale configuration (मा च त्वं) ending conclusively into अंजलिकुर्मि and रामस्य माऽधर्मो मामिह स्पृशेत.

It is possible to observe that the reception of an equivalent through the creation of idealised variants is a worthy situation that occupies an order of importance in the Structuralist discourse. It has to be admitted that the property of acquisition intentionally revives the configuration of a composite structure and hence the association remains an important principle of construction inasmuch as it leads to the creation of multiple absolutes which are in turn considerd to be so necessary for the exact identification of variables within the artistry.

Artistic form, to a great extent, is the process of modification inasmuch as ideal structure is not forthcoming, and, because of this, the exact condition of the holistic content and configuration is not known. A substantial part of this structure opts for renewal of figuration through division and substraction so as to bring about an addition of further content.[21] Division is, in structuralist terms, a manner of progressive reinvention based on compulsory restructuring of less enriched part by completely removing the terms which are anti-formative. Both Saussure and Jakobson observe one of the instances of necessity of the fact in the following remarks. Saussure states:

> Language is a system whose parts
> can and must all be considered in
> their synchronic solidarity. — 87

Jakobson would similarly suggest the following condition of conjunction:

> Any unbiased, attentive exhaustive total description of the selection, distribution and interrelation of diverse morphological classes and syntactic constructions in a given poem surprises the examiner himself by unexpected, striking symmetries and anti-symmetries, balanced structures, efficient accumulation of equivalent forms and salient contrasts, finally by rigid restrictions in the repertory of morphological and syntactic constituents used in the poem, eliminations which, on the other hand, permit us to follow the masterly interplay of the actualised constructions. — 603

It could be seen that strength of signification conceived, created and produced in the formation of a perceptible sequence of value and order is facilitated when the primary categories cohere around a fixed and determinate code. In this regard, it would be wise on our part to make mention of the fact that the contradiction of corresponding opposite figural form enhances the possibility of union, yet each of the values has to

---

21. The motif of transformation has its foundation in the synthesis of the constructs of language, like, for example, language becomes construction when it opts for a growth in terms of addition, multiplication, division and subtraction. For further description on the subject, see Culler.

be routed through either a contrast or division so as to bring forth the most enriched form. In Saussure's contention the whole situation acquires a manner of collective and continuous growth, while in Jakobson's the idea is immediately active and creative of an instance of proposition. To subtract is to cancel the overlapping part of conformity so much so that the resultant shall have a determinate form and function. This is not to say that the excess of value is marked inessential, it is rather infused into the actual content expansion. There are two major types of ways for subtraction and division that we are trying to expand as a worthy principle of resolution of an object into an event: (1) by compound initiation and (2) contorted induction. In each of these, it would be really remarkable to understand how the synthesis of content is facilitated only by approving and allowing segment of the two most enriched and authentic variables to come across and form a valid scale of meanings. In Saussurian system, composition of content would intend and manifest homogeneous and heterogeneous forms of alliance inasmuch as the origin of value as a source of signification is rooted in both static and evolutionary forms of the functioning of a word. For this reason, any word variable marked as *A* shall have a primordial form *a* while it would also in the due course of time give rise to *A* and *a*. Saussure does not insist on the fact that the origin of word and the creation of meaning constitute differential proposition, while, on the other hand, the determination of meaning is a matter of a fixed and conceptually sound scheme of evolution.[22] Under any circumstances, accordingly *A* will have to sustain the extent of synthesis only by retaining its place and position in *A* and

22. In a system of grammar suggested by structuralist poetics, the sound variants also occupy considerable manner of consideration. For further description on the subject, see Saussure.

A. For example, look at the Sabhāparva of the *Mahābhārata*:

भीम उवाच –
भवन्ति मेहे बन्धक्य: कितवानां युधिष्ठिर।
न ताभिरुत दीव्यन्ति दया चैवास्ति तास्वपि।। – 129

bhīma uvāca —

bhavanti mehe bandhakyaḥ kitavānāṁ yudhiṣṭhira ।
na tābhiruta dīvyanti dayā caivāsti tāsvapi ।।

Here we could understand that position of words intends a continuity of replacement, and, therefore, the positive function of determination is equal to the negative function of intra-determination (inasmuch as it accounts for rejection of the substantial part of cumulation of synthesis. For this reason the opening is made through an interrogative inquisition (भवन्ति मेहे) and the same is thrown open for the sake of inception of multiplicative inquisitions synthesised in prospective time sequence and, therefore, we have two major figural forms of inquisiton (भवन्ति, दीव्यन्ति) and four imminent modes of improbable indetermination (कितवानां, ताभिरुत, न चैवास्ति and तास्वपि). It could be seen that reasolution has, in principle, a configuration around seeming probability derived from the structural forms and configuration which could be represented in the following manner:

Σ (युधिष्ठिर) = A^+ (भवन्ति मेहे) = A^- कितवानां = Axa (ताभिरुत चैवास्ति)

= A ÷ a (दीव्यन्ति दया)

Laxical determination through improbable and probable replacement could be termed to be as an important part of meaning creation in the above verses, and, for the similar reasons, the structuralist interpretation offers a significant form of artistic comprehension and understanding and the worth of which has already been detailed in the foregoing explanation.

Structuralist poetics confers a unity of organisation on the methodical as well as figurative contents in such a way that there is a constitution of theoretical proposition as a part of rapid, immediate and endless synthesis that is promoted by accomplishment.[23] On the other hand, the intensity of appropriate sequencing of resolvable object and resolvable subject becomes so rich in variation and proportion that the condition of participating models, contents and the categories becomes symmetrical and conjoint. This exercise is one of the best modes of value creation among the enriched contents and the structures of conjunctions, which induce the process, are invariably addition, multiplication, association, subtraction and division. In each of these, as we have suggested the extent of transformation is governed by the intensity of artistry conceived in the medium and the context.

The interpretative forms and propositional structures developed in structuralist situations leads to the creation of a valid basis for the determination of timeless and temporal events. Hence myth and metaphor remain two compulsive orders of situations that will call for valuation and assessment.

VI

Metaphor is a process of rearrangement of empirical necessities and empirical reality associated with the resolution of an object into event; hence, it carries the formal encodings of the

---

23. The activity of figures of speech in the manner of organisation and modification of the artistic formation could at once be understood in the form of the logical stretch of the underlying evolutionary contents. In the structuralist poetics, figural forms are in fact the different indices through which coordination of an artistic formation proceeds and is also simultaneously accomplished. For further description on the subject, see Genette.

categories and this presents them in the form of models.[24] The conception of metaphor presupposes a correspondence of configuration between a determinate object and an indeterminate subject and a determinate subject and an indeterminate object, and, at the point of interception of the both, we can understand the creation of metaphor. It is remarkable to understand that the construction of a value structure presupposes an ideal form, and, for the same reason, there is a good deal of refinement of medium and context. In the structuralist tradition, metaphor has been considered to be as synthesis, modification or rearrangement. Accordingly, it is carried out through an established procedure of reconstitution, in which, a category is exposed to a series of indeterminations by inventing the figures of correspondence which are in themselves inexact and inappropriate, yet are capable of identifying the terms of correspondence and reversibility. The length of reversibility suggests a framework or a model with regard to the displacement and relocation of the time as an event, and, for the similar reason, a metaphor can be considered to be as a triangular structure investing substantial portion of extension in adjusting the intensity of refinement of the categories. Existence of metaphor forms two important artistic conditions. In the first place, it generates the method of correlation and in the second it invents the nature of transformation of an object into an event. Correlation is basically an intention to assist the conduct of suggestivity as a part of the achievement of reality in the formal presentation of resolved categories.[25] Obviously, the question

24. Figures of speech undergo committed and sincere mutation through a logic and sequence. Metaphor, for example, is a rich function of sign formation. For further description on the subject, see Culler.

25. The assertion made by the contents explicates the virtue of necessity of correlation among the categories, hence facilitates the process. For further description on the subject, see Culler.

of indifferent reception may arises because the generative content and the regressive content are lacking in the orientation to extend the conjunctive part. The extension of meaning that invents a purpose of modification is accordingly subjected to so many deviations and digressions and because of this the stretch of content may not obtain an exact suitability, as is required to be, in developing the requisite compulsory codes. Saussure for example, observes:

> (1) Of a dissimilar thing that can be exchanged for the thing of which the value is to be determined; and (2) Of similar things that can be compared with the thing of which the value is to be determined — 115

In the development of the units of expanded correlation the precision would ultimately rest with the emergence of series of internal and external concentrated forms and it could be arranged obviously by changing the relative positions. Accordingly, the resulting construction shall have an upward and outward extension or stretch of the form. In building up the length of unit, the contents are moved in a progression, and, therefore, the combination is exactly fitted into each other so that the entire figure becomes very compressed. Saussure could suggest that preliminary inversions do not either intend or even incorporate the vertical or horizontal mass of denotation. In fact, the extent of reference is lengthened for the purpose of addition of the resultant fact. Thus the reception of content is brought about to a realistic assertion. It can be stated that in a metaphor, the suppression of content becomes the exposition of value so much so that the denotative mark is recreated into empiricism of correlation and ultimately it becomes an instance of preferential or selective mutation. Barthes, for example, explains the situation in the following manner:

> . . . are subjected to rules of combination or composition. These rules would easily permit a formalisation of the erotic language, analogous to the 'tree structure used by linguists . . .

> In the Sadian grammar there are two principle rules: there are, as it were, regular procedures by which the narrator mobilises the units of his 'lexicon' (postures, figures, episodes). The first is rule of exhaustivity: in an 'operation' the greatest possible number of postures should be accomplished simultaneously. . . The second is a rule of reciprocity . . . all functions can be exchanged, everyone can and should be in turn actor and victim, fluzellator and flazellated, coprophazist and coprophagized, etc. This rule is central. — 34, 35

According to Barthes, the advancement of a figure is suggestive of the progression of unit within and on that account the prospective correspondence authenticates a term for an activity in the morphological as well as semantic formation, hence the meaning unit is conceived. We can see that there are at least four suggestions involved in it. In the first place, the progression of a form does not immediately lead to the assortment of values, rather it would be deferred till the time the contents within are symmetrically revived. Secondly, order of perception and suitability of functioning are similarly conjoined in a similar scheme. Hence the resultant figure is not divested of the motives of preference. In this way the growth of correlated meaning would be, at the same time, formation of an intensity of combination. The third and fourth consequence presented by Barthes will have its relationship with the inverted value-equivalent in the whole situation. The selection and presentation of progressive units would render the growth of the object and the subject almost anew. This scheme to express with commitment and sincerity could be better understood in the following verses of Sabhāparva from the *Mahābhārata*:

त्यजेत सर्वां पृथिवीं समृद्धां,
युधिष्ठिरो धर्ममथो न जह्यात्।
उक्तं जितोऽस्मीति च पाण्डवेन,

तस्माद् न शक्नोमि विवेक्तुमेतत्।। – 121

tyajeta sarvāṁ pṛthivīṁ samṛddhāṁ,
yudhiṣṭhiro dharmamatho na jahyāt ।

uktaṁ jito 'smīti ca pāṇḍavena,
tasmād na śaknomi vivektumetat ।।

In these verses, the presentation of object and subject is in the manner of correlation proposed as a necessary part of the reinvention of systematic, careful, concentrated, reasonable, precise and authoritative formation of the function contained in the artistry of the above situation. The verses open up as a note of an advice to the agitated Pāṇḍavas at the sight of injustice and non-intervention, therefore "त्यजेत" extends the terms of correlation and proposes an affirmative sequence of mutation. In this verse we can identify the object "युधिष्ठिर" and the subject "धर्म" being brought closer for an extraordinarily discreet amalgamation. The correspondence of the object and the subject is in the manner of inception and therefore every act of correspondence inducts a motif of transformation as well and with every transformation we can realise how the contents and the subjects are obviously placed in conformity with the strength of correspondence and therefore the expression त्यजेत सर्वां पृथिवीं समृद्धां। युधिष्ठिरो धर्ममथो न जह्यात presupposes a process of reinvention of primary into secondary and for that matter context into content. The exercise of presentation builds up an assurance to the creation of semantic and morphological interrelationship in the text, and, for the same reason, the achievement of correspondence and correlation as parts of the invention of metaphor follow structuralist paradigm.[26] There are two reasons to be prescribed for this method in this act: (1) the order of

26. Morphological and semantic congruence brought about by topological activity must sustain the ethics of modification. For further description on the subject, see Greimas.

significance (पृथिवीं समृद्धां and धर्म) necessarily puts forth value significance in respect of each, therefore, finally the idea of विवेक्तुमेतत् is a reality. The formation of metaphor would obviously remain a recovery of the origin, expression and growth of object as object and subject as subject. The primary form of an object is precisely what is conceived in the structurality of the earliest terms. For this reason the recovery of a word originally situates a figure in synthesis. In the structuralist circumstance, the position of an object is, of necessity, the one that is defined through a regular change in the manner of denotation and for the purpose word is intentionally distorted to the extent that the injunctive part is notionally equal to the length of extension suggested by the distortion. We can formulate a perspective for an interpolative and interactive procedure adopted to supplement the strength of extension in the creation of a metaphor, and, for that matter, we have to approve the idea that expansion of a word because of the correlatives of the word, would never enter into direct modification; it would rather commute the relative functions for the sake of forming a direct coordinate of transformation. It is to be remembered that to change the perspective of the immediate configural form is to enhance the qualitative function of harmony and precisely because of this the emergence of product carries the primary form of relevance. Saussure states:

> (1) A new class of words, proposition, was created simply by shifting the existing units. A particular arrangement, which was originally of no significance and came up probably by some chance, allowed an altogether new grouping: kata, independent at first, was united with the substansive Óreos, and the whole was joined to baino so as to serve as its complement. (2) A new verbal class (Kalabaino) appeared. This is another psychological grouping, also favoured by a special distribution of units and consolidated by agglutination. (3) A natural consequence, the meaning of the genitive ending (ore-os) was weakened — 180

As is suggested by Saussure, the condition of figure and attitude of the content towards induction of appropriate form to validate the adequacy of proposition is to be considered as one of the important objects of lengthening of the meaning apparatus, while, however, in the cases in which distribution of content is randomly persuaded, we can understand and observe the total transformation being achieved as a part of the structural plan and hence synthesis. In fact, Saussure is examining the possibility of inward exchange of the corresponding richness and weakness of the letters or syllables or words. It is because of this reason that the proposition of change in the morphological set-up is sometimes not adequate to the historical urgency of identification. Saussure would also like to examine the point as to how the inversion of a syllable over the period of time has quite carefully supplemented the generation of a word on the whole. In the structuralist tradition on the whole, the idea of metaphor is appropriately understood to be the condition of: (1) displacement of the context, (2) assortment of the content, (3) modification of the medium, and (4) transformation of subject and object and in either of the cases the emphasis is on the creation of a heterogeneous version of semantic network in which phonetic, morphological and semantic relations prepare a thoroughgoing continuity and on that account, metaphor is nearly a concrete universal; for example, the following passage from Donne's "Ascension" would enable us to fecilitate an understanding of the situation:

> Salute the last and everlasting day,
> Joy at the uprising of this Sunne, and Sonne,
> Yee whose just teares, or tribulation
> Have purely washt, or burnt your drossie clay;
> Behold the Highest, parting hence away,
> Lightens the darke clouds, which hee treads upon,
> Nor doth hee by ascending, show alone,
> But first hee, and hee First enters the way. — 1-8

In these verses Donne creates the mode of value by emphasising the necessity of significance inasmuch as the content of formation and the content of correlation are nearly the same. The idea of abundance at the sight of the achievement of purity as a canonical principle could be attributed to the primary content that displays the case of relationship between the object and the subject. In this particular context, the poem conceives a union/synthesis/transformation/transmutation of object into subject inasmuch as the timeless event in the form the God (sunne) and the temporal and material thing (sonne) have now become one and all, and therefore, principle of purity has now been established (lightens the dark cloud). The consequence of joy is felt in the formation of reason as one of the objects of conceptualisation, and therefore, the poet expresses with profundity and says "Salute the last and everlasting day". The principle of comparison that has been adopted by the poet lies in the extraordinary/precise rearrangement of the contextual forms, accordingly, there is great a displacement of the signifiers and for that matter each signifier evolves into the totality of value. For example, "Salute the last" is a term of noteworthy designation composing adequate precision at both the ends. Salute confirms and adjusts the relative sequence of opposition between the primitive anguish and agony of being caught up in the eternity of life and death. Exposition of metaphor to constitute a direct term of discretion concentrates the process of conjunction, therefore, "sunne" meaning the everlasting and "Sonne" conferring the material standard of understanding the world, are really the constructs, which advance the effect of correlation. From the structuralist perception the conduct of the metaphor in this particular passage is purely obtained from value relationship obtained through conformity and inception, as is evident from the following:

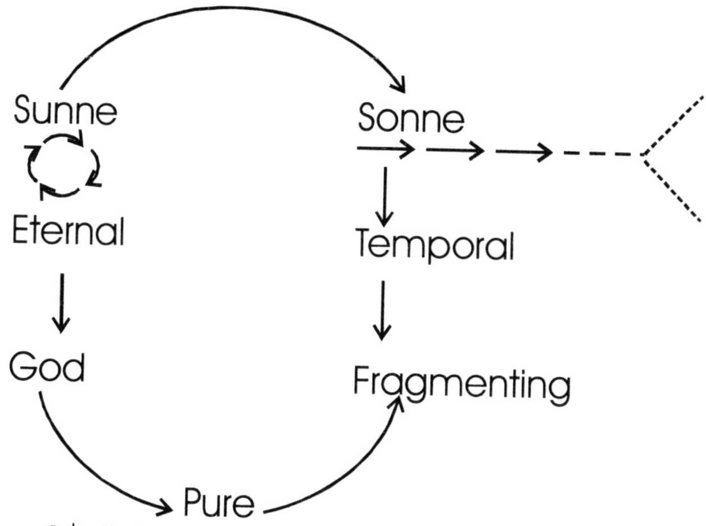

$$A = A^{+} + A^{-}$$

The complementary nature of the assertion of the value enjoined upon "Sunne" and "Sonne" forming truth in a valid binary opposition is the situation that extends the meaning for the further association and interrelationship. At any structure of time, it could be seen that "Sun" indicates a cyclical version of the significance attatched to the moment perceived in supra-rationalisation while "Son" consciously concludes the length of time. So far as the poet's relationship with the situation is concerned, he insists upon a comparison with the both — Sun is a form of eternity therefore "Gods" incarnation and "Son" is once again a form of material conduct and illusion meaning only death.

In the structuralist interpretation, John Donne befits the evolution on account of the fact that creation, placement, replacement and displacement are the basic motives around which the extension of subject-object relationship must be made to extend and in this context there is a point in justifying such an exercise.

The growth of an artistic situation brings about so many compulsive orders of comprehension, and, for this reason, modification of the medium and transformation of object into subject could be cited to be as examples of the fact.[27] Roland Barthes explains the whole issue in the following terms:

> The work is not surrounded, nor designated, nor protected, nor directed by any situation, no practical life is there to tell us what meaning we must give it . . . however prolix it may be, it possesses something of the concision of the Delphicoracle, its words conforming to a first code (the oracle did not ramble) and yet open to several meanings, because they were uttered outside any situation, except the situation of ambiguity itself. . . .
> — 58

The purpose is conclusively established that the force of the works upon the content is something that also derives the exact and real position of figures lying within the object. In this context, the interpretation offered by Roland Barthes is well worth consideration and it has to be made a point that configuration of the context, on occasion, yields to open-ended correlation and the effect of which is felt in the substance of resolution formed as a part of the continuity in expansion. The nature of metaphor is evidently a possibility and reality that is effected from this particular part of the framework, while the exceptional growth in coordinates of concentration of artistry becomes almost a principle, purpose and motives and moreover the forthcoming addition to the object in the background of changing context is also an area of meaning that has to have a first-hand recognition. The substance of proposition realises on the method of inquiry conducted via the wholesome structure of the object and the subject and the

27. The notions of functionality, growth and evolution are so necessary to the Saussurian principles that the idea of language is imminently juxtaposed in the ideal forms that it would explicate for itself. For further description on the subject, see Saussure.

necessary relationship that the underlying medium has with the exact figure of correspondence. Change of object would mean the conversion of both index and identity while change in the manner of subject structure would essentially convey the idea that definite position of form has undergone a kind of perceptible variation in a manner in which the segmental devisions are thoroughly appropriated. The next important step that goes into a series of objective and concrete divisions in the artistry, is appreciably inducted through the synthesis of medium. Medium is an instrument to restore the higher models of expansion; therefore, change of medium for the sake of synthesis definitely intends the creation of newer and richer forms of equivalents for each of the artistic relations that occur as a rule between various figures interposed in between. For example, look at the following verse from Donne in "A Nocturnall Upon S. Lucies Day":

> But I am by her death, (which word wrongs her)
> Of the first nothing, the Elixer growth;
> Were I a man that I were one,
> I needs must know; I should prefere,
> If I were any beast,
> Some ends, some means; Yea plants, yea stones detest,
> And love; All, all some properties invest;
> If I an ordinary nothing were,
> As shadow, a light, and body must be here. — 28-36

In this, Donne considers, examines and evaluates the prospects of obtaining and proposing a course of evolution for resolution into a necessary truth of existence, and, for this purpose, the transformation and mutation of the first person is remarkable. From this foundation, he proceeds to examine the necessity of bifurcating and separating the general individuality and universal individuality, and, therefore, resolves to exclude every purpose as being insignificant and every motive, every attitude, every aim and every principle as being untrustworthy except that the self of the poet must extend beyond and include the larger self of the beloved and the synthesis thus obtained will have to be the final meaning of the existence. In this, the opposition between medium, context and the content is very important. The context appropriates the position of signifiers inasmuch as each of the words puts forth an index for its own sake, and, in the second place, each index becomes suggestive of a large-scale interrelationship derived from the indices themselves.[28] For that matter the word "Elixer", "Sunne", "Goat", "Summer", "Festival" graduate along an evolutionary scale of enrichment. It has to be accepted that Donne is quite successful in bifurcating the length of evolution and extent of evolution by simply composing an organic system of the revival in which object-subject relationship is extended till the time the last stretch of meaning is available, therefore, the mortality of wordly forms and functions bear comparison with canonical wordly effects constituted in sun (decay of the rays by evening), goat (short-lived and inconstant posture), festival (short-lived joy). The mark of signification is actualised in the configuration of proportionate value obtained in key indices and therefore the composite whole emerges towards the end where Donne states with conviction "let me prepare towards her", and "let me call/this house her vigil, and hers, since this/both the ears, and the days deaf, midnight is".

VII

In Ānandavardhana's term of perception, the constitution of metaphor is imminent in the creation of *dhvani* for the growth

28. Commitment and urgency for the sake of meaning are the illustration of the creation of concrete forms; because of this, in structuralist poetics, sometimes contents are realised through the small universe that they create, and once again emphasis would lie on the utmost functionality of every sign inherent in the words under consideration. For further description on the subject, see Barthes.

of an ideal artistic situation.[29] Accordingly, the definition of metaphor envisages an approach towards re-estimation, revaluating reinterpretation and re-examination of primordial as well as functional categories. To this extent the term metaphor would obviously mean development of the point of interception derived from the assorted expansion accorded to the participating models and categories. For this reason *śabda, pada, vākya, bhāva, vibhāva, sthāyībhāva, anubhāva,* and *sañcārībhāva* are brought to enact the necessity of this procedure. Eventually, as Ānandavardhana would suggest, each category (those mentioned above) would construct advancement for concentrated location of the universal in itself. The growth in such a manner fixes up and determines the creation of a wholesome object of meaning in which application and organisation of the semantic configuration is accordingly adjusted and verified. In these terms, applicability of metaphor is larger than any posterior or anterior form of meaning inasmuch as the form of function so obtained is consciously appropriated to manifest meaning in all its possible variations.[30] Thus, the emergence of universal accommodates the function of meaning in semiotic, morphological,

---

29. Metaphor is one of the greatest facts of synthesis of the enriched categories. In *dhvani* the concept and tool of metaphor could be best explained by upgrading the emperical contents and rationalised construction. Accordingly, it is obtained at the point of interception of experience and reason. For further description on the subject, see Ānandavardhana:

    रूपकादिरलङ्कारवर्गो यो वाच्यतां श्रितः।

    स सर्वो गम्यमानत्वं विभ्रद्भूम्ना प्रदर्शितः।। – 2.26

30. The role played by metaphor in generating a conscious tool of realisation of reality in the background of intending truth is creative of excellence in transformation. Consequently, metaphor is an instrument of transformation. For further description on the subject, see Mammaṭa:

    अलङ्कारोथ वस्त्वेव शब्दद्यत्रावभासते।

    प्रधानत्वेन स ज्ञेयः शब्दशक्त्युद्भवो द्विधा।। – 4.38

phonological as well as semantic contents. The appropriateness of effect, by the standard of constitution, upholds the principles of an ideal artistic creation.

Ānandavardhana in *Dhvanyāloka* explains the nature of such a discourse in the following manner:

अर्थशक्तेरलङ्कारो यत्राप्यन्यः प्रतीयते।
अनुस्वानोपमव्यङ्ग्यः स प्रकारोऽपरो ध्वनेः ।।

रूपकादिरलङ्कारवर्गो यो वाच्यतां श्रितः।
स सर्वो गम्यमानत्वं बिभ्रभ्दूम्ना प्रदर्शितः।।

अलङ्कारान्तरस्यापि प्रतीतौ यत्र भासते।
तत्परत्वं न वाच्यस्य नासौ मार्गो ध्वनेर्मतः।। – 2.25, 26, 27

arthaśakteralaṅkāro yatrāpyanyaḥ pratīyate ।
anusvānopamavyaṅgayaḥ sa prakāro 'paro dhvaneḥ ।।

rūpakādilaṅkāravargo yo vācyatāṁ śritaḥ ।
sa sarvo gamyamānatvaṁ bibhrabhdūmnā pradarśitaḥ ।।

alaṅkārāntarasyāpi pratītav yatra bhāsate ।
tatparatvaṁ na vācyasya nāsau mārgo dhvanermataḥ ।।

Ānandavardhana holds the position that the process of explication and mutation of the categories and the models are sometimes generative of upward mobility and sometimes of downward progression while these perfect the process of reception of the contents into external models. It would suggest a configuration for each of such participating events and towards the end of this event there would be an altogether new form of category or model that would be taken as a standardised external referent for the actual concretisation. In the downward mobility of the system, the categories and the models are infused into each other and together they move towards the coherent absolutes. Eventually, there is a coalescence of these two factors rendering them to organise and authorise the various components of the artistic situation for the sake of enrichment. The contentions put forth by Ānandavardhana have relieved the necessity of focusing primarily on the formal content in such a way that both, the emotive and linguistic functions are brought to conformity with the fact of universal. In these terms of signification, the emphasis is entirely on the following ideational figures: (1) metaphor is a substance of universal, (2) metaphor, being organic, constitutes a manner of lengthening the relationship of the transformation, (3) because of both of the above factors metaphor is an absolute, (4) inasmuch as exercise of formation of relationship is continuous, the possibility of having the meaning is open till the generic or generative universal is obtained, and (5) creation of metaphor is an approval of comprehension, valuation, evaluation, and interpretation of the participating figures of speech, therefore, the continuity of discovery of a model is infinite and endless.

Ānandavardhana expounds the idea that the figures participating in the process of artistic creation have the immediate necessity of compounding the method of conjugation. In fact, it would appear as if the idea of correspondence and ability of a figure to introduce the textural author for the sake of appropriation of an exact body of correlative to constitute a framework for the meaning. In this regard, two things appear to be quite imminent. There must be a prior enrichment of the functions inherent upon every category and, in the second place, the refined version of the model that one gets is brought to further universalisation.[31]

---

31. The process of idealisation begins when the natural form of *śabda, pada, vākya, bhāva, vibhāva, anubhāva, sañcārībhāva, sthāyībhāva* are designated along a conclusive injunction. What comes up in consequence is the concentration and from this the figural poetic truth seems to be emerging. For further description on the subject, see Abhinavagupta:

स्वं स्वं निमित्तमासाद्य शान्ताद्भाव: प्रवर्तते।
पुनर्निमित्तापाये तु शान्त एव प्रलीयते।। – 3.26

What is significant about the whole thing is that Ānandavardhana insists on a careful selection of the model and afterwards a thoroughgoing introduction of a set of conjunctions to the advancing model, and finally, the process of transformation that would make the model under consideration a part of the larger universe of semantic, morphological and semiotic appropriateness. This must be understood to be a distinction accorded to the fact of rationalisation by a full-length and full-scale inculcation of emotive as well as verbal figures. At any point of time, in an artistic situation, the necessity of conceiving an emotive model undergoes uncertain assertions in that the projection and synthesis that they are made to be carrying, are not rightly and rigidly contextualised in the advancing medium. Accordingly, we can comprehend that there is a misappropriation of a category and method of insertion of a model into the context, content and medium will have to be the part of priority the poet should accord, and accordingly, once the process of refinement is over the purified category/ model has to be transferred to the next equivalent with an equal fairness. Mammaṭa in *Kāvyaprakāśa* advances the concept and holds the following position:

वक्तृबोद्धव्यकाकूनां वाक्यवाच्यान्यसन्निधेः ।
प्रस्तावदेशकालादेर्वैशिष्ट्यात् प्रतिभाजुषाम् ॥

योर्थस्यान्यार्थधीहेतुर्व्यापारो व्यक्तिरेव सा ।
बोद्धव्यः प्रतिपाद्यः। काकुर्ध्वनेर्विकारः। प्रस्तावः प्रकरणम् ॥ – 3.21, 22

vaktṛboddhavyakākūnāṁ vākyavācyānyasannidheḥ ।
prastāvadeśakālādervaiśiṣṭyāt pratibhājuṣām ॥

yorthasyānyārthadhīheturvyāpāro vyaktireva sā ।
boddhavyaḥ pratipādyaḥ । *kākurdhvanervikāraḥ* ।
prastāvaḥ prakaraṇam ॥

Mammaṭa examines the relationship and interrelationship between the object and the subject as determined by the extension of object to appropriate determinants like the speaker, person spoken to, intonation, the sentence, the expressed meaning, presence of another, context, place and time. For that matter, the excellence of an object as object would lie in the fact that it could transform each of the above situations into a new whole and thereby would carry the conviction that a universal form has been established containing the truth of the situation. In this, we can invariably understand the importance of two significant situations. Mammaṭa proves the point that the creation of effective discourse in an artistic situation could be the result of the process of the growth of inquisitive model within the categories, and for this purpose, the association between the object and the subject or subject and the object is of great importance. In the object we have authoritative inherence of the value, while, on the other hand, in the subject we have the actual correlatives which may derive themselves from the generic nature of primordial association. Accordingly, there would grow and develop a point of interception when the categories would be induced for the sake of comprehension. In each such effort the position of value would exactly be at the medial position. In fact, the assertive occupants and the expository occupant of the process of correlation consciously cohere together and give rise to a truthful form of meaning function in which the focus is not exclusively on semantic assertion; there is rather a tendency to include every inner and every outer extension of formation.[32] Thus, the constituted meaning becomes a grown-

32. The principle of association in *dhvani* follows the manner in which contextual adequacy corresponds to the strength of the medium, as a result of which propriety is obtained. For further description on the subject, see Ānandavardhana:

क्रमेण प्रतिभात्यात्मा योऽस्यानुस्वानसन्निभः।
शब्दार्थशक्तिमूलत्वात्सोऽपि द्वेधा व्यवस्थितः।। – 2.20

up function for the reality of the whole artistic situation. Mammaṭa's emphasis is on the extended order of the elevation of semantic function so as to include context, content, medium, transcontext, transmedium and transcontent could explain how the adequacy of both, the internal and external correlatives is eminently justified to occasion the presentation of the best order of truthful communication. On the whole, Mammaṭa could be understood to have supported the explication of the following intensive/extensive variations:

1. Comprehension of the concrete universal in the artistry involving identification, discovery, selection and expansion.
2. The orientation of the categories for the sake of inverted rationality.
3. Transformation of the thoroughly signified units.
4. Expansion of primordial forms to the source of universalisation.

Metaphor in Indian context is viewed, as a figure of advancement of upward coordinates of expansion and accordingly the idea of evolution is not entirely ruled out. It would mean that the primitive function of concentrated form is equal to the developed function of the refined form. Because of this, the validity of comprehending the context implanted into the workings of two forms would be really the necessity to expose valuation of the situation to external hypothesis. This in turn would help in forming a series of applicable models right at the place at which a form of semantic association originated. Ānandavardhana in *Dhvanyāloka* describes the situation by implicating content and context in an extensive correlation and observes:

यस्त्वलक्ष्यक्रमव्यङ्ग्यो ध्वनिर्वर्णपदादिषु।
वाक्ये सङ्घटनायां च स प्रबन्धेऽपि दीप्यते।।

शषौ सरेफसंयोगो ढकारश्चापि भूयसा।
विरोधिनः स्युः शृङ्गारे ते न वर्णा रसश्च्युतः ॥

त एव तु निवेश्यन्ते बीभत्सादौ रसे यदा।
तदा तं दीपयन्त्येव तेन वर्णाः रसश्च्युतः ॥ – 3.2, 3, 4

yastvalakṣyakramavyaṅgayo dhvanirvarṇapadādiṣu ।
vākye saṅghaṭanāyāṁ ca sa prabandhe 'pi dīpyate ॥

śaṣau sarephasaṁyogo ḍhakāraścāpi bhūyasā ।
virodhinaḥ syuḥ śṛṅgāre te na varṇā rasaścayutaḥ ॥

ta eva tu niveśyante bībhatsādau rase yadā ।
tadā taṁ dīpayantyeva tena varṇāḥ rasaścayutaḥ ॥

It is quite obvious from the above statement that the acquisition of a property for the sake of value in the linguistic model would correspond to the simultaneity in the intensity of generation of idealised content in the equivalent phonetic and morphological conjunction obtained in each of such formations. It is, therefore, quite necessary that the internal correlative should be so highly expanded that it could develop similar means of propagation. Furthermore, the actual application of the ideas is more relevant than the strength of cohesion and synthesis. Look at the following example from Shakespeare:

Mine eye hath play'd the painter and hath stell'd
Thy beauty's form in table of my heart:
My body is the frame where in't is held,
And perspective it is best painter's art:
For through the painter must you see his skill,
To find where your true image pictur'd lies,
Which in my bosom's shop is hanging still,
That hath his windows glazed with thine eyes.
— Sonnet XXIV

In the above Sonnet the commitment for the sake of correlation is exactly fixed up by making out a proper display of the visible strength of the artistic situation. To elevate this methodology, the poet introduces the term "painter" and thereby enlarges the qualitative condition, both by multiplying the contents and adding the contents. In fact, every effect succeeds the largest formal arrangement contained in the idea of the painter. "Painter" is the God who controls the method and function of arrangement of order in this world, and, for that matter, oversees everything from beginning till the end. In this the suggestive function is particularly noted in the word "painter" for carrying the reality of truth beyond the primordial formation. The range of correlatives obtained in "painter" is significant, and, for this reason, it appeared in an extraordinarily heightened form with lateral conjunctions all-around. Interplay of associated correlatives is also excellently reorganised with the help of rapidity of transformation achieved between the object and the subject, and the subject and the object. It appears as if the length of focus constituted in the "painter" inscribes the application of both, the visual and deceptive formations. The consistency impinged upon the "painter" is absolutely constitutive of a mode of explicit communication in which the arrangement and order are insisted upon. In that way the formation of *vivakṣita* in the "painter" by explicating and introducing a set of pattern to substantially engage the larger figures of enrichment is almost absolutely intended, and, accordingly, the extraction of metaphor could be at length presupposed.

The strength of appropriate selection of the categories for the sake of the creation of a stable order of the content, could be the reason, why a larger part of the synthesised content is virtually added to those figures, which are about to be transformed into an absolute term. Accordingly, it must be understood that the generation of comprehensible units would eventually give rise to a coordinated system of functions. The applicability of models in this respect would be twofold. In the first place, each of the categories would acquire an extensive network of enrichment, so much so, that the acquisition of new content would automatically invent supreme form of reasonableness and this will go till the time parallel order, equivalent order, parallel function and equivalent functions are made to cognise into each other and this extraordinary function of enrichment would give rise to a figure in the form of metaphor. Morphological advancement, in this regard, begets a series of additive forms and each such form in turn constructs a universal for itself. This happens to be one of the important occasions to find out how and why the expansion of the grammatical, phonological and semantic form is acquired. Pāṇini in *Aṣṭādhyāyī* obtains an interpretation by suggesting the following methodology of addition:

वृद्धिरादैच ।। – 1.1
vṛddhirādaica

Pāṇini proposes to obtain a form of synchronised contents in which there would be a constant and regular upgradation of the foreground and background of the construction of any organised referential apparatus. With this intention, he invents the property of motivated expansion in which all the primary terms and all the secondary terms and nearly all the associated terms would be conjuncted, through the process of transmutation and, from each, therefore, a significant term would come up. This could be seen to be as one of the great advancements ever achieved by any theorist, and, out of necessity, it projects the intention of creation of a figure whose relations and interrelations are adequately, appropriately and exactly sustained. Even otherwise, the worth of consistency entrusted is of high significance and it immediately leads to the conclusion that the primordial, phonological, morphological and semantic forms invent a degree of association, and accordingly, they proceed to exclude the association for concrete universals to be obtained in consequence of such a progression.[33] The other important result that is of great worth considering objectively, is the nature of the following equative arrangement:

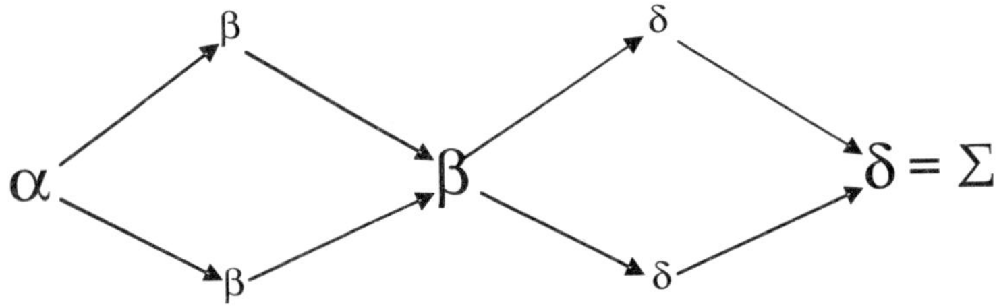

The arrangement of contents, in accordance with the given projection, would follow the sequencing in the manner of assorted transformation comprehended through the reinvention of binary formation. This is an authoritative advancement supported and suggested by the actual coherence consolidation and conjunction of the categories. The category of metaphor, accordingly, is a situation of presentation in which the binary function of the same categories comes to be routed till concentrated index is thoroughly brought to the communicative network in the artistic situation.

The approach of significance and substance in the creation of this form results in the succession of the idealised content. As a matter of fact, the length of object and the form of subject, both are associated in such a way that each is in a position to presuppose the validity of the forthcoming context as the homogeneity or heterogeneity are consistently inducted into the formalised system. Viśvanātha in *Sāhityadarpaṇa* explains significance of such a situation in the following words:

33. The insistence on progression, generation, substantiation, comprehension, explication and realisation of both value and function, is very pragmatic in the manner of its conception. It helps in composing an authority for grand artistry. For further description on the subject, see Hockett.

अनेकार्थस्य शब्दस्य संयोगाधैर्नियन्त्रिते।
एकत्रार्थेऽन्यधीहेतुव्यञ्जना साऽभिधाश्रया।। – 2.21

anekārthasya śabdasya saṁyogādhairniyantrite ।
ekatrārthe 'nyadhīhetuvyañjanā sā 'bhidhāśrayā ।।

Viśvanātha makes it quite clear that the concentration of expansion of the content in one direction is only an impossibility. Thus, the direction of the progress of meaning is absolutely qualified where denotation yields the significance of suggestion, and from that function, one could understand how extraordinary level of significance is intended for the sake of the creation, rather than a formal figure being designated as metaphor. Viśvanātha insists and attributes the consistency of qualitative performance brought about by the acquisition of the right place, right context and right time for the distortion of the one of the contents, indicating a possibility for association and correlation; that is how, it might be possible to understand how the concrete intentions are at once obtained and realised, while the artistic forms are developed in accordance with the necessity of generative function suggested and implanted within.[34]

In the following verses of Kālidāsa in *Abhijñānaśākuntalam* the induction of qualitative significance of experiential motif and linguistic form suggest universalisation of the truth as one of the forms of signification:

राजा (सस्पृहम्)
चलापाङ्गां दृष्टिं स्पृशसि बहुशो वेपथुमतीं
रहस्याख्यायीव स्वनसि मृदु कर्णान्तिकचरः।

34. Correlation could be understood to be as a concrete evidence of a change of medium in which proposition is essentially the consequence of realisation. For further description on the subject, see Vāmana:

गरुशुश्रूषया विद्या मधुगोष्ठया मनोभवः।
उदयेन शशाङ्कस्य पयोधिरभिवर्धते।। – 3.19

करं व्याधुन्वत्याः पिबसि रतिसर्वस्वमधरं
वयं तत्त्वान्वेषान्मधुकर हतास्त्वं खलु कृती।। – 1.23

rājā (saspṛham)

calāpāṅgāṁ dṛṣṭiṁ spṛśasi bahuśo vepathumatīṁ
rahasyākhyāyīva svanasi mṛdu karṇāntikacaraḥ।

karaṁ vyādhunvatyāḥ pibasi ratisarvasvamadharaṁ
vayaṁ tattvānveṣānmadhukara hatāstvaṁ khalu kṛtī।।

The presentation of the object conforms to the strength of an attitude as an idea and that is exactly what we could understand to be primarily functional in the utterance of Duṣyanta. Thematically, the event is related to the longings of Duṣyanta in not being able to meet Śakuntalā; he therefore becomes anxious, impatient, enraged and the like. And, to add to his anxiety, the whole nature is coming into Śakuntalā and blessing her. The cricket is singing a song; coocku is also prolonging her song; bees are humming and dwarfing their flights. Now it appears to Duṣyanta as if he is being deprived from the realisation of the grandeur of the beauty of Śakuntalā while all others are keenly attending on her. In this, what is to be observed, is the concentration of an idea as an occasion to suggest the formal and authoritative function of correlation. In fact, when Duṣyanta says "चलापाङ्गां दृष्टिं स्पृशसि बहुशो वेपथुमतीं" he proposes to extend the ideational effect of correlation by identifying the sensations as the principle even of conception. The projection of the content is in the manner of evolution of the sensation, and therefore, the utterances such as "कर्णान्तिकचरः, पिबसि रतिसर्वस्वमधरं"and also तत्त्वान्वेषान्मधुकर find out the basic nature of realisation of an understanding of the emotion. There are at least certain forms, which could be said to be very important, for example, वेपथुमतीं and तत्त्वान्वेषान्मधुकर supplement the process of expansion by rationalising the content of suggestion. For this reason, the metaphorical activity in the whole passage is keen on finding out as to what object is purported for the sake of an explicable variant of sensation and what context is the most appropriate for the revival of the primacy of sensation. Taken together, these two words suggest the manner of conceiving the truth of beauty and the beauty of truth. On the other hand, the empirical equivalence of the signifiers and sign could enlist a clear and exact term of meaning. This could be proved by making a point that चलापाङ्गां and रतिसर्वस्वमधरं, both are intentionally and contextually suited to perform the function of signifiers so as to bring forth the signified contained in तत्त्वान्वेषान्मधुकर.

In *dhvani* tradition, metaphor occupies a significance of primordial content offering a full-length artistry and, therefore, it is comprehensively motivated through experience, language and intellection and the complete assortment of each into each could find a way out of the conventional framework of the entire artistic situation. It is also because of this that the idea of metaphor, having the ability to illuminate and flash forth everything, holds good in that the content, context and the medium are put and proposed for the sake of an emergence into a new empirical form.

VIII

The appropriate constitution of the text as an object of exposition and realisation is one of the principle aims of *dhvani* and the structuralist poetics.[35] In the structuralist poetics, the idea of evolution of language into meaning with the attendant experience and inherent structures supplement the process of the generation of thoroughgoing textual condition. By text, we mean an organised form of literary discourse, where the

---

35. It would be interesting to find out how *dhvani* and the structuralist poetics combine in themselves an authentic evidence of addition, multiplication, division, and subtraction to create a concrete universal so as to obtain truth for linguistic and emotive functions. For further description on the subject, see Ānandavardhana and Saussure.

nature, form and function of language and experience are evolved and established as complete systems, and the worth of the whole is utilised for the sake of comprehensibility leading to precise realisation. While, on the other hand, in *dhvani* system, the generation of the text is the basic premise of the evolution of the categories and on that account words, letters, syllables, paragraphs, *bhāva, vibhāva, sthāyībhāva, anubhāva, sañcārībhāva* undergo complete modification by inventing a degree of graduation within themselves.[36] In other words, it could be said that assortment as an independent body of transformation constructs an index of identity amongst the categories in such a way that each is capable of holding up the finally refined contents. For that matter, text could be the function of movement coherently incorporated by actual terms of effect. In both the traditions, the condition of textuality is also the principle of synthesis and evolution of the empirical categories.

In *dhvani* system, the composition of text or body of discourse is meant to be having a scale and length of evolution from the primary form to the utmost universal model. Yet, with the changing degrees of assertion and intensity the varying instances of artistry with primordial centre are observed. It would mean that the identity of language is wholesome inasmuch as it is created out of the total effect

---

36. Of the three possible divisions of *dhvani,* namely, *vivakṣitavācya, asaṁlakṣyakrama* and *citra,* the intensity of correspondence between emotive and linguistic categories and subsequent evolution of each into each becomes the object of concern. *Vivakṣitavācya* is held to be the highest for the reason that the correspondace, evolution and transformation are absolutely full-length and full-scale. For further description on the subject, see Mammaṭa:

अविवक्षितवाच्यो यस्तत्र वाच्यं भवेद्ध्वनौ।
अर्थान्तरे सङ्क्रमितमत्यन्तं वा तिरस्कृतम्।। – 4.24

inherent in *śabda*, *varṇa*, *pada* and *vākya* that is congregated through simultaneous cognition and proportional transformation. The event of enrichment is precisely determined by the fact that the models constituting the language like *śabda*, and *pada* are themselves precisely synthesised that they could associate all the preceding and succeeding contents with an intentionally appropriated method.[37] Ānandavardhana could understand that the final emergence of discourse in a system of artistry is to be explained by symmetry, harmony, purity, elegance, precision, organisation and finally the truth which are essentially the products of the growth of language and experience in a system. While the situation is exactly what Ānandavardhana makes mention of, it is possible, on the other hand, to expose certain terms for appraisal of the situation. The coherence of discourse along the coordinates of precision follows a normative procedure of designated and identified sequencing of the whole situation.

In *Dhvanyāloka*, Ānandavardhana is of the opinion that the aspects of comprehensibility developed in the categories are required to be successfully transformed and ought to be uniformly felt and distributed all along the discourse. He says, for example:

---

37. The evidence of an appropriate context is furnished in accordance with role orientation provided for the sake of change from the primary to the secondary situations. This carries a concentration of excellence for each of the participating categories. For further description on the subject, see Paṇḍitrāj Jagannātha:

कर्पूर इव दग्धोऽपि शक्तिमान्यो जने जने।
नमोऽस्त्ववार्यवीर्याय तस्मै मकरकेतेव।।
स एकस्त्रीणि जयति जगन्ति कुसुमायुधः।
हरतापि तनुं यस्य शंभुना न बलं हुतम्।। – 2

वाच्यानां वाचकानां च यदौचित्येन योजनम्।
रसादिविषयेणैतत्कर्म मुख्यं महाकवेः।।

रसाद्यनुगुणत्वेन व्यवहारोऽर्थशब्दयोः।
औचित्यवान्यस्ता एता वृत्तयो द्विविधाः स्थिताः।। – 3.32, 33

vācyānāṁ vācakānāṁ ca yadaucityena yojanam ।
rasādiviṣayeṇaitatkarma mukhyaṁ mahākaveḥ ।।

rasādyanuguṇatvena vyavahāro 'rthaśabdayoḥ ।
aucityavānyastā etā vr̥ttayo dvividhāḥ sthitāḥ ।।

It is clear from the emphasis that the creation of discourse in artistry is based on the constitution of idealised condition and on understanding of language, and, at the same time correct contextualisation of an experience. It would further mean that there should be a position to comprehend the sensation in such a way that the effect of sensation is equivalent to the force generated by the equivalent words.[38] On the other hand, Ānandavardhana also upholds the principle of sanctity of value obtained in language and experience, and accordingly, he could say that the chronology of value must be fixed and determined in an appropriate sequence justified by the strength of content, context and the medium. It is possible to understand that Ānandavardhana supports a condition in which the function and determination of elementary situation and significant situation are purported to be obtained as the part of the process of evolution and it must be the method to induct and adopt corresponding changes in the structure of the categories.

---

38. Poetic excellence is unquestionably the matter of the upbringing of reality as a part of the expression of the experience. Accordingly, a good poem is one in which the instrument of rationality intervenes and upholds the consistency of various models created in the poem. For further description on the subject, see Dhanañjaya:

कस्यचिदेव कदाचिद्दयया विषयं सरस्वतीं विदुषः।
घटयति कमपि तमन्यो व्रजति जनोयेन वैदग्धीम्।। – 1.3

The wholeness of the contents so achieved and so thoroughly distributed along every coordinate of synthesis and order that the artistry has out of necessity become specific to the universal forms. If we look at Ānandavardhana's observation, we could understand that he is laying emphasis on an artistic discourse that has the following characteristics:

1. The text is principally the creation of the correspondence and synthesis of the categories, which are involved in the exchange of the content as a rule.
2. The ideal state of transmutation achieved by the different categories is also the mark of the creation of the text.
3. The existence of sequence presenting harmony and order could be substantially the length of the extension of concentrated expression.
4. In *śabda, pada, varṇa, vākya*, the principle of conformity, correspondence, order is obtained by an appropriate sequencing in such a way that every displacement at the completion of enrichment would cause subsequent inception for the sake of renewal of such a process. On the other hand, with regard to emotive categories like *bhāva, vibhāva, sthāyībhāva, anubhāva, sañcārībhāva* similar emphasis in the rotation and mutation of the models is observed.

It is, therefore, the prevalence of an ideal artistic situation, characterised by the full-length and full-scale concretisation of the categories that is also simultaneous with the creation of text in the work of art.

The motif of creation, exposition, synthesis and the modification of an object into event is one of the principal ways to effect the condition of resolution of primary into significant forms of linguistic and emotive experiences, is at the bottom of *dhvani* and structuralist tradition of inquiries.

In *dhvani* system, the creation of an ideal artistic situation is brought about by an invention of appropriate structure in terms of language and experience. Thus, the units of language like words, letters, syllables and the whole paragraphs and units of experience, like sensation, imagination, emotion, feeling and thought are made to comprehensively situate themselves in an extraordinarily concrete environment, and, accordingly, once the procedure and effect along the situation is comprehended, the transformation of each of the units of language into each of the models of experience is realistically brought about.[39] This is one of the stages in which the mechanism of transformation follows the principle of relative, cumulative and superlative manner of modification, yet, in each case, absolutely concrete form with linguistic and emotive constructs is obtained. One could immediately understand that the manner of conversion of an object into event is synonymous with the inculcation of appropriate structure of language inherent in *śabda*, *pada*, *vākya*, *bhāva*, *vibhāva*, *anubhāva*, *sthāyībhāva* and *sañcārībhāva*. Having discovered appropriateness in terms of each of these, the duty of the poet is to activate his *pratibhā* (refined sensibility) in such a way that graduation of language and experience till an appreciable period of time becomes possible. The point of interception at which refined language and refined feeling could cut each other is created and exactly at that point, the highest poetic sensibility suggesting genuine artistic environment is conceived. In making an estimate of such a system one could understand very well the progression of the categories could always presuppose a correspondence with the similar constructs on the emotive side of the situation, therefore, the manner of construction of effect also leads to

---

39. The functionality of *śabda, pada, vākya* along with equal purification of *bhāva* and other categories remains in process through which identity as a part of relative event is determined. For further description on the subject, see Bhartṛhari.

the consideration of addition, multiplication, division so on and so forth. The act of placement and organisation of the units, parts, models, and constructs in this particular system present the extent and magnitude of coherence and reasonableness, so much so, that each factor is brought to a remarkable extent of refinement. The extent of conception of reasonableness inherent in a category is substantially what the scale of universal could intend for such a purpose. Ānandavardhana presumes that the beginning of an effect of appropriateness in the language and experiential formation with the artistic system is, in fact, also the beginning of an act of constitution of realistic contents, realisable terms and a comprehensible variety of artistic association. To effect such a manner of precision, there are, as suggested by Ānandavardhana, three stages of transformation. In the first place, there is a correspondence of refined constructs with the equally refined contents, and, secondly, there is accumulation of the process leading to large-scale contextual and medium specific changes in the whole system. The progress of artistry towards authoritative and reasonably universal orientation is thus a scheme that could be adopted via sequence of method, terms of structure, effect of modification and restoration of concrete universal in the approved model of significance. In *dhvani,* the concretisation of each of these for the sake of an assorted significance is so high and so great that every native form that inscribes a configuration of absolute total and functionally absolute content is comprehensively the reality of resolution. Any artistry that becomes complete in terms of figuration, fixation, exposition and determination of the participating models and categories is intended to commit itself to the prospects of large-scale effects based on the adequacy of cognitive contextualisation and refinement, and, in each, this should be a development of organic function through external and internal correlation and association.

The growth of artistry from the elementary incoherence to secondary universality in itself approves of the fact that the conduct of transformation and expansion of resolution has two basic events. It has compound and the generative forms embodied and hidden in morphological, semiological, semantic and phonological attributes. The extension of even one of these procures similar and identical changes in the terms of actual strength of the character. Thus the consequence of disposing a word for the sake of an experiential form becomes intent of the high artistry. In fact, it seems to be better to state that *dhvani* precisely confirms appropriateness in the constitution of categories and models on the basis of internalised, externalised discretion. Figure in a category, for example, sensation in a word carries the supra-abundance of arithmetical as well as geometrical terms. On that account, addition of one coordinate with the other must be based on precise configuration intended in their direction of movement and to calculate the measure of that movement the synchronisation of all the directions into one direction is principally motivated. *Dhvani* factually confirms the process of exaction in this regard. There is yet another way of finding an illustration of the orientation and configuration of the artistic categories, and, for that matter, there is a careful and coordinated working of equivalent for the sake of growth of the categories towards wholeness. Ānandavardhana insists on the induction of one principle effect so as to synchronise and synthasise all the minor effects which could be cited as an evidence of the fact that from the bottom the movement of enriched content continues upwards till the time it reaches the highest level. This is, really a novelty that introduces a new method in literary scholarship whereby one understands how the exact and the absolutely purest versions of synthesis are the basic realities of this type of artistic situation. Everywhere in the artistry the function of presentation shall always be equal to the depth of exposition. Thus the inclusion of supra-developed constructions is unquestionably the strength of the theory. To facilitate this process, Ānandavardhana speaks of a typical mechanism of graduation, envisaging full-scale modification of the participating categories, and, for the purpose, he could understand that every *śabda, pada, vākya, bhāva, vibhāva, anubhāva, sañcārībhāva* subsists and subsumes a concrete universal in the content so that they purport to uphold for the purpose of refinement and to complete the event of absorption into their immediate universal forms. The authority of construction of the figures calculated to generate a condition of exact correspondence between the enriched *śabda* and the enriched *bhāva* resolves the immediate background and accordingly turns all the categories into a conducive network, foreseeing the creation of a total and complete artistic formation. In structuralist poetics, the manner of constructing an artistic form is based on the presumption that every formation conceives and anticipates the form of association and correlating the unit and part of the categories tending to be wholesome on their own account or by an act of interdependency generated in the purity and refinement. To this extent, the idealisation would intend the creation of a thoroughgoing textual apparatus with noteworthy consequential formations like homogeneous and heterogeneous organic codes in the form of society, culture and religion.[40] The condition of creativity that comes to be at the foreground of formative concern is typical of the constantly evolving substances, objects, events, conditions, situations and the like. It is, thus, the achievement

40. Even otherwise, in larger emotive associations, namely the cultural and religious formations the workings of the structuralist poetics are very much evident. In religion and culture, the constitution of coherent symbols leading to a definite signifier acts as a necessary presentation for the sake of value and meaning. For further description on the subject, see Saussure.

of cumulative, relative, interactive, supractive, and immediatly correlative, contra-relative, intra-correlative conditions of the growth of function in the categories. In fact, the formulation of an event or situation or object is presumed to be comprehending a systematic and coherent distribution of codes, variables and indices identified as artistic agents and consequently each is produced through a calculative term of expansion. It is evidently assumed that every artistic formation intends an immediate and supra-immediate universal, designated as text within the enlarged authoritative mediums of textual existence. Thus primary text or primary artistic form, hypertext or hyperartistic form and hypoartistic extensions are also quite noteworthy in this regard.

The occasion of advancement of a category in structuralist understanding is by evolution in which full-length and full-scale genesis is placed at the causation of the entire event and because of this primary scale of enrichment it is decidedly different from the secondary terms of conjugation. An advanced formation of structure must induct the ability to make an evidence of concrete relations in the artistic situation. On the whole, the structuralist tradition identifies the categories on the basis of their propriety of configuration and Saussure, Roman Jakobson, Roland Barthes and Lévi Strauss have advanced the seminal idea in relation to concentrated activity observed in phonological and morphological, phonetic and semantic divisions.

In *dhvani* and the structuralist tradition of constituting and comprehending artistry, the configuration of artistic formation with an emphasis on isolation, identification and evolution of the linguistic and emotive categories are emphasised for attention. In *dhvani*, for example, the creation of categories (*śabda, pada, varṇa, vākya, bhāva, vibhāva, sthāyībhāva, anubhāva* and *sañcārībhāva*) is both, the deductive and inductive process. The structure is precisely based on the manner of the concretisation and also the intensity of correlation that must be inculcated as a rule to substantiate the entire framework. Every category is intended to generate a matrix of large-scale and small-scale effects and each large-scale effect is expected to become a concrete universal with an ability to intensify the process of cognition. There are two events which are normally associated with the growth of absolute artistry in the background of committed correlation brought about by linguistic form and emotive events. Thus, *śabda* on the one hand, *artha* on the other, could produce an exceptionally rich, enriched, precise and refined order of contents to propagate the progress of artistry successfully and without any impediments and obstacles. *Śabda* is presumed to be an order of rationality through which every event is brought to a projection at a realistic enlargement or expansion. On this ground it can be stated that sequence of formation of significant forms and significant relations within the linguistic segments would adequately be supplemented by such a situation. Ānandavardhana, Mammaṭa, Abhinavagupta and others have held that the causative effect of *śabda* is always greater than even the series of synthesis obtained relatively in other forms participating in the same act of evolution of artistry. Especially Ānandavardhana suggests that the figurative content and the fixed content of an artistic form must independently intend an aspect of purity for themselves and there should be the correspondence between the improved model at every succession and also at every juncture. It would mean thereby that the categories are positionally as well as situationally cognised in order that the wholesome cognition would bear the mark of its predecessors. The scheme of arrangement will have to be in the manner of downward succession and upward accession and this class of movement is mainly creative of concentrated effects to promote the intention of form within the content and content within the form. The idea of the generation of the text as a material form suggesting the higher order of universal function like truth, ideal so on and so forth, become the comprehensive realities when such a situation is expounded to bring about ultimately that the *śabda* is a reality and this proceeds to significant dispersions of the reality through constant changes in the condition of its power to relate, interrelate and correlate. Going by the authority of Pāṇini and Bhartṛhari, Ānandavardhana upholds the fact of the reversibility of *śabda* in the sense in which it is in a position to expose the refined categories to the outer environment so as to imbibe the suggestive factor situated therein. The style of progression as developed in Ānandavardhana's view of the matter is an exceptionally rich presentation of the idea of conformity and equivalence. While it seems to be a part of complete situation, it could also bring to our notice the characteristic of *śabda* as one of the native facts of configuration. The internal network of idea, intention and content orientation brought about by *śabda* is an authentic proof of the fact that the area of projection and synthesis is comparatively larger when *śabda* is conducted in a favourable artistic environment. The necessity of such an event also corresponds to the acquisition of purely indivisible versions of the participating models, and the quality of induction supports the view that any term and any condition of idealisation begins right at the exact option for comprehensibility provided by the *śabda*. There might not be sometimes accidence of overgrounded and overactive configuration leading to the absolute in the formal alliance. Thus, in *dhvani*, the condition of displacement effectively revives the necessary dimension of appropriate form and appropriate content. The idea of appropriateness in relation to the creation of total artistry is so elevated and so advanced that external figures like metaphor, metonymy, synecdoche, simile, assonance, alliteration and internal semiotic and phonological constructs become independently cognised to the extent of infinity, and, therefore, the presentative function of enrichment is always directly proportional to the creative form of adaptation. In an artistic formation, the consequence of a cause and resolution of an effect are so intentionally significant for the sake of each other that the interpretative and assimilative forms become radically substantiated and strengthened.[41] The idea of *dhvani*, thus, significantly situate the immediate as well as forthcoming configural models for the sake of universal effect considered to be so necessary in keeping with the worth of an artistic situation.

In the structuralist poetics, on the other hand, the substance of categorical forms like language, experience, thought, imagination, presuppose the formation of conjunction, injunction, coordinates and variables, both at the level of the text (generative, constitution) and also at the level of an external reality termed as hypertext in compassing the value determinants of any cultural system. The orientation of the linguistic units like word, letter, syllable is supposed to be purely formal to an extent that the correspondence and conjugation built around the two categories would be typical in the manner of quantifiable and isolable units of construction. It is with this end in view, Saussure extends the argument that language and meaning essentially reciprocate each other in the background of a chain of signifiers mooted in each of these. The development of language for the sake of an artistic form is immediately the simultaneous revival of certain determiners through which the language adopts the associative

---

41. In the artistic formation, rationalisation and ratiocination are the events occasioned by the ability of the categories to appose the content and context. The distinction of enrichment brought forth in each of the conjugal categories is so much so that opportunity for the sake of universalisation becomes essentially a reality. For further description on the subject, see Mammaṭa:

    अनुस्वानाभसंलक्ष्यकमव्यङ्ग्यस्थितिस्तु यः।
    शब्दार्थोभयशक्त्युत्थस्त्रिधा स कथितो ध्वनिः।। – 4.37

function. Thus, a word is morphologically significant only because of the fact that it carries the abundance of numerous and many historical as well as completely semantic antecedents within itself. This confirms the view that the strength of any linguistic unit is proportional to its emotive function, precisely in the manner in which the emergence of both is presupposed, in an appropriate ideological and ideational background. From this perspective, it would be convenient to divide structure of any form into completely homogeneous relations through which an enriched version of heterogeneous and reliable artistic formation is conceived. This, therefore, is adequately a complete reordering and restructuring of the strength of the forms and the categories.

In Saussure, one has the necessary projection of formative situation that guides the creation of the expository units of the language, and, therefore, word, letter, syllable, sentence could, out of necessity, conform to the extraordinary mutation of the similar forms carrying a greater range and length of values. Accordingly, every word inculcates and situates harmony of signifiers through which the function of meaning is concluded. This would further mean that the word is made to dispose itself for the sake of infinite range of possibilities to be realised in the domain of value. The later structuralists like Roland Barthes, Roman Jakobson, Greimas, and Genette have brought forth the necessity of upholding linguistic and emotive categories as if every unit of a category and every unit of an experience is substantially in a position to yield to consequence, should an effect be allowed to resolve them in proximity and in vicinity. This goes a long way to suggest that the effect of modification of one category on the other is obtained immediately if the sequence and manner of the signifier intends direct, relative, and cumulative value perception simultaneously and at once. In this perspective, we can understand how the resultant text conceives a range of interdependent segments and we can quite conveniently refer to these as being hyperactive text, hypostatic text, hyperstratified text and hypotext. In either of the conditions, the richness and excellence of the native form, like the word, the letter, the syllable adopts the primary as well as secondary function of meaning lying in the whole situation. Roland Barthes suggested that distortion of a word could simultaneously be the process that would lead to the greater function of meaning generation inasmuch as every act of proposition and cognition is ultimately qualified, decided and determined by the immediate perception of the significance suggested by the same word for the sake of an appropriate order. In the structuralist tradition, the function of the proportionate category is suggested by comprehending rather a greater range of stylistic similitude spread over an immediate cross-section of substance and the ideas. There can be two stages to determine and disperse the situation. In the first place, the artist could work out universal models based on the condition of truth that they generate, and, secondly, the process of restructuring has to start with collateral connection with the immediate textual conditions opting for the synthesis. The development of category as model in the manner of interpretation is not exhausted until a regularity in the magnitude of value is figured and conceived. To build up an authentic structure of meaning, the movement of letters and syllables should be prefixed and suffixed around the bottom of an index, which should also be, at the same time, an idealised condition of presentation of the content and context to the external space. It would mean further that the categories shall have to follow the path of expansion in both, the idealised internal artistry and empirical external world. In this, the twofold division would imminently put forth the prescription of an evolutionary scheme for the sake of refinement. Accordingly, Saussure inculcates a method whereby he could examine the substance of the word in relation to immediately preceding content as well as multiple, manifold and various external coordinates through which purport of meaning enhanced value is extensively realised. For a word to be specific as a condition of generation, there will have to be adequacy of correlation and proposition, hence, the movement and displacement for word is obtained in consequence of the similar advancement of content towards the order of authenticity in the ideational network. Such a view establishes at once and through the condition that the form of any major system (say, for example, epic in poetry) could induce the generative content only the basis of a thoroughgoing preceding and succeeding context and the order of such a function will establish the motif of an idea as a substance in the resultant product. At any instance of time, the worth of such a situation completes the intersignificational gaps observed in producing the sequence of contents. The precise interplay of the linguistic and the emotive contents form simultaneous, continuous, continual, congruous perception of harmony, both in internal and external divisions of the art. Jakobson and others have approached the qualitative measures rooted in the advancement of the categories towards noteworthy and designated enrichment. Thus, he could view the matter with an emphasis on linear propagation through specified models acting as the instruments of transformation for the sake of signification. The units of language progress and correspond to an approval in the hands of a modified receptor and thus the beginning of progression is content-inducted.[42] This conformity to the sequence specific unit is one of the conditions of creation of an ideal artistry.

In *dhvani* and structuralist poetics, the ideational events and relative forms, functional constructs and universal forms

42. The process and period of evolution of language are basically very slow in nature, and, on that account, sufficient time is gained for the discursive appropriation of the contents. For further description on the subject, see Culler.

are contained within the absolute reality of the medium and context and it is because of this situation that appropriateness indication is a part of the creation of a distinct, clear and a forthright sequence intending both the substance and reason for the growth of an artistic situation. In *dhvani*, for example, the method of creation of a category (*bhāva*, *sthāyībhāva*, *vibhāva*, *anubhāva*, *sañcārībhāva*) is by the adoption of adequacy of the given situation to its immediate context, thus relevance of *bhāva* could be made to situate itself on a necessary intensity of refinement. Thus the logic of perception as well as apprehension and recognition propose stylistically rich perspective for the whole situation. Ānandavardhana suggests that constant replacement of the ordinary by significant, refined by crude, and particular by universal must, at the same time, be an event of total presentation of facts and substance related to the artistic situation. It is, therefore, the *bhāva* that undergoes correspondence and inducts a term of language for itself. It has to have a place and role in the relational systems of progression and invention. On this basis, we can deduce the fact that place and situation of a category like *bhāva* would be resultant of a greater and idealised form of artistry, if the correspondence with reasonable substitute is realised as a possibility of transference. This event is active in all the circumstances that come to attend the creative inception. In fact, every pursuit that intends to raise the possibility of enrichment is also universally disposed to functionalise every term, every content and every unit so much so that the result of the effect is absolute of the whole system.[43] The idea of

---

43. Authority of convergence is precisely a figural excellence in which complete modification is not only assured but also made to be generously progressive. For further description on the subject, see Vāmana:

धम्मिलस्य न कस्य प्रेक्ष्य निकामं कुरुङ्गशावक्ष्याः।
रज्यत्यपूर्वबन्धुव्युत्पत्तेर्मानस शोभाम्।। – 1.22

transformation is, thus, something that makes its appearance both at the beginning and at the end of an artistic situation. Going by the observations of Ānandavardhana and the interpretation of *dhvani* suggested by the commentators, we can understand that transformation is effectively a process of concept generation and the generation of the concept is appropriately figured in number of segments and multiple authorities of graduation of the categories along the symmetrical lines. It has to be conceded that object of inquisition and motif of preference, both are made to conform to the actual intensity of configuration, and, for that matter, the worth of an idea in the form of meaning that is generated after the formal modification of the contents is the embodiment of totality as such. Ānandavardhana examines the whole event by relying on the concept of universality of the artistry as obtained in each of the events of transformation. He authoritatively made mention of the fact that the system of artistry is to be made excellent only by substantiating different universals found in different orientations. For this reason, we can have *śabda* and *artha* as the proportionate division of universal function. *Śabda* is an extent of sufficiency obtained in the generation of elaborate system of reason orientation and reason expansion. Thus any *śabda* that happens to commute itself to the function of artistry ought to be in a position to functionalise the entire situation. Ānandavardhana's explanation in this regard seems to be a ground for the growth of purpose of object intention at the most primordial level. Revival of the figures of extension through systematic and proportional organisation could be understood to be at the bottom of transformational situation developed in the arguments put forth by Ānandavardhana and the commitment to the conduct of function will have to be noticed in the poetical circumstances, and for the purpose, consider the following verses of Andrew Marvell in "To His Coy Mistress":

Let us roll all our strength, and all
Our sweetness, up into one Ball.
And tear our pleasures with rough strife
Through the Iron gates of life.
Thus, though we cannot make our Sun
Stand still, yet we will make him run. — 1-6

In these verses, the prospects of assertion and intensity of intention, both are situated in the eventual concretisation of *śabda* and *artha*. We can understand that the verses open on a note of declaration of a statement suggesting truth of the matter. For this reason the strength of a word enjoins upon the power of multiplication and addition, and, thus, with the first declaration (let us) the contents begin to emerge. The word *roll* and *strength* act as the different phases of correlation through which the rise of metaphor in *sweetness* is understood. *Sweetness*, for that matter, is suggestive of the note of pleasure (the physical pleasure) thus the effect of same is expanded simultaneously with the event of correlation. It is also possible to say that the note of distinction applied intensively on all the words adds to the property of conjunction and because of this the strength of such words as *sweetness, tears, pleasures, let us roll, iron gates,* is immediately understood. The argumentative function of the word is combined with the exact emotive configuration. This primarily is responsible in the genesis of refined artistry. And, on the other hand, the process of idealisation continues additionally with the advancement and prolongation of the word "strength", meaning strength and, at each of the stages, it would always be open for us to note the point that the associative content and generative categories have together built up the excellence of artistry and thus the case of *dhvani* is substantiated. To work out a theory of *dhvani*, it is sometimes felt that the cause of advancement of a given content in a given poetic situation may not necessarily be based on the presupposition of idealised situation. Accordingly, a word or group of words would create the wholesome situation without any specific notation provided for every term occurring in the process. This must be viewed as one of the ideational strengths of the immensity of logic and reason contained in the system.

The movement and displacement and also replacement of the context and content so as to generate a condition of rationality are also at the back of the structuralist poetics. The operative function of a word and the semantic inversion inducted into the system explain the reality and substance of formal principles adopted in the structuralist conception of the ideal artistry.[44] The introduction of the word at any stage is also, at the same time, a creation of value-necessity in the given situation, and subsequently, the projection of the highest intensity of the resultant meaning is also relationally pursued. It would amount to saying that every word ultimately is signified and every signified, on the other hand, is quite naturally a word. This adoption of the scheme of evolution of a word into the signified and every signified into a word is in itself illustrative of the consequence of change. One has to understand that the interplay of word and signified, and signified and word, illustrates the circumstance of modification and resolution of the contents. This issue would presuppose certain manner of application and for the purpose consider Bhavabhūti in *Uttararāmacaritam*:

लक्ष्मणः – (रामं निर्वर्ण्य साकूतम्) आर्य, किमेतत्?
अयं तावद्बाष्पस्त्रुटित इव मुक्तामणिसरो,
विसर्पन्धाराभिर्लुठति धरणीं जर्जरकणः।
निरुद्धोऽप्यावेगः स्फुरद्धरनासापुटतया,
परेषामुन्नेयो भवति चिरमाध्मातहृदयः।। – 29

---

44. The depth of artistry in structuralist condition anticipates the formation of completely assorted models with a great reliance on evolutionary principles. For further description on the subject, see Sturrock.

lakṣmaṇaḥ — (rāmaṁ niravaṇya sākūtam) ārya, kimetat?
ayaṁ tāvadvāṣpastruṭita iva muktāmaṇisaro,
visarpandhārābhirluṭhati dharaṇīṁ jarjarakaṇaḥ ।

niruddho 'pyāvegaḥ sphuraddharanāsāpuṭatayā,
pareṣāmunneyo bhavati criamādhamātahr̥̥dayaḥ ॥

Here we can understand that the sequence of the words and their order, both replace each other and create a distinct framework of an absolute system in which symmetry between word variable and signified content are almost to the extent of being universal. The agony of separation and lamentation for not being able to revive the primitive proximity are at the bottom of the exhortation of Lakṣmaṇa in *Uttararāmacaritam*. What is important, according to structuralist inception of the situation, is the scheme of signifier adopted and cyclical function of sign invented by the dramatist. The constitution of agony and lamentation of Śrī Rāma has been projected through a distance by Lakṣmaṇa thereby intending an addresser-addressee relationship. In fact, implicated signifiers obtained in tears, flowers, rivers, lips and the heart could compound the situation to be formally juxtaposed in an ideal sequence. Thus वाष्प, मुक्ता, मणि, धरणीं, स्फुर and हृदय: could constitute paradigmatic functionality of the signification. It is always conspicuous that वाष्प foresees a construction of an absolute thereby it would recquire only a minor displacement to construct a formal position of order in मुक्ता, मणि and these taken together would obviously prepare a ground for a strength of the total signification suggested by चिरमाध्मातहृदय:. The immediate situation that inscribes the formulation of a totally cognised content is explicated almost at the middle of the several lexicons. Thus मुक्ता and मणि are medially signified by the virtue of the fact that actual sound is deciphered through an equivalent code contained in the semiotic mark that it creates. Accordingly, the sorrow, grief, suffering, agony and longing distinctly mutate the controverted implication. It has to be clear that every term of signifier multiplies with the addition of exact value, therefore, equivalents becomes extremely remarkable. For example, look at the following scheme:

तवद्बाष्पस्त्रुटित	=	मुक्तामणिसरो
विसर्पन्धाराभिर्लुठति	=	जर्जरकण:
निरोद्धोऽप्यावेग:	=	स्फुरद्धरनासापुटतया
परेषामुन्नेयो	=	चिरमाध्मातहृदय:

Implication obtained in the advancement of such a position is rightly felt to be the creation of maximum contents to order a formal index of concentrated signifiers. In structuralist interpretation, the order of sign has to mutate the relevance of the signifiers inasmuch as the words or the letters, which create the signifiers, are themselves generated in the immensity of this possibility.

The strength of categories obtained as units in *dhvani* and structuralist poetics invents a notion of heterogeneity in performing morphological, phonological, semiotic and semantic functions. It is precisely in this context that Ānandavardhana introduces *śabda, pada, varṇa, vākya, bhāva, vibhāva, sthāyībhāva, anubhāva, sañcārībhāva, ālambana, uddīpana* as the necessary commitments towards constructing and composing universal functions for the sake of idealisation of an artistic situation. The act of commitment aggravates the necessity of determinate and aggressive content formation, irrespective of the content and the medium in which they were generated. Thus *śabda* is capable of developing the evidence in favour of implication and explication and would accordingly generate a series of correspondence with emotive form situated in *bhāva, vibhāva, sthāyībhāva, sañcārībhāva* and the like. In these conditions the manner of being externalised and internalised would olso be known at the same time. The focus, therefore, is on applying a condition of necessity of content-admission, content-proliferation, content-elongation and content-modification. Once the structure in consequence of such an intention is obtained, the creation of an absolute of artistic form is immediately accomplished. While one looks at the selective nature and function of emotive order, one is really conscious of the fact that every inducement in this regard is necessarily something that would add to the growth of an evidence, substance, reason, idea and hence truth of the entire form. Ānandavardhana sees how the aggregate of compound conjunction could be the suitable ideal for constructing a methodical and realistic presentation. *Bhāva* is essentially an effect of totality, and therefore composes every functional and dysfunctional orientation of the categories towards a necessary synthesis. The views adopted by Viśvanātha, Ānandavardhana, in this regard, would suggest that *bhāva* tends to purify the substance of the experience and obtains an absolute model for presentation. There are certain ways in which an exclusive movement of presentation of the substance is taken to be as cumulation of all the necessary endorsements of the content.[45] In this regard, the effect of *bhāva* is felt to be both, combinatory and multiplicatory, and also completes the index and sequencing of the content in a proper assortment. In Abhinavagupta's view the intensity of idealisation is an evidence of the fact that the process of purification is complete and the emergence of an impersonal variant is now a reality. Viśvanātha also understands *bhāva* in the manner in which it is regulated by the authenticity of functional proportion and is creative of an absolutely indivisible position. The

45. It would always be the matter of systematic presentation rather than being anything else that would lend figural and formal strength to the consequence of observation. For further description on the subject, see Bhāmaha:

शब्दाभिधेये विज्ञाय कृत्वा तद्विदुपासनम्।
विलोक्यान्यनिबन्धांश्च कार्यः काव्यक्रियादरः।। – 1.10

constitution of effect that attends to the growth of *bhāva* would invariably indicate how an artistry could be appropriately moulded for the sake of purity, indivisibility, wonder, impersonality and the like. Every conceivable movement on the part of the content is also the prolongation of the concrete assortment of inherent artistic substance, therefore, proportion, symmetry, harmony, order are situated rightly at the centre of everything that conceives the *bhāva* as an instrument. The other universal descendants of *bhāva* like — *sthāyībhāva, vibhāva, anubhāva, sañcārībhāva, ālambana, uddīpana* could also effectively promote the consequence of substance and idea. The appearance of *bhāva* as an object of reality, therefore as the model of signification, is understood to be the excellence of interpretative modification examined and purported in the Indian literary theories. The question of propriety of creation of a term intending significance upholds the validity of the effect of constitution in *bhāva*. The method is to sequence the logical parts and to terminate the deviant conjunction. On the whole, one will have to conceive the fact that the ideal artistry at any point of time shall constitute a relative intention of significance with the universality of the categories under consideration and to synthesise the categories the preparatory functions are coordinated in the *bhāva*. The other categories like *sthāyībhāva, vibhāva, anubhāva, sañcārībhāva* are also equally designated in respect of their capacity to induce the strengthening of external and internal aspects of the artistry. In *dhvani*, the completion of appropriateness in terms of categorical presentation has a primary notion of exact configuration. Thus in *sthāyībhāva*s, the reality obtained in the external world is apprehended and recognised till the time it is suited to the reality of the artistic situation. To that extent, *sthāyī bhāva*s supplement both the converse and inverse of the process of construction. In other words, we can say that amalgamation is the necessary note of exposition and the act of amalgamation itself would bear the idealisation of the whole situation. Similarly, *vibhāva*, and *anubhāva* as the two realistic orders of synthesising procedures to make out a fact of significance by universalising the external formation or by internalising the contents in the eternal order.[46] In either of these situations, the preparation of correlations to transfer and communicate objects, situations, events, subject, forms and even individuals is so absolutely simplified that the worth of harmony and proportions is immediately obtained.

In the structuralist system, the constitution of an idea and the experience are effectively persued in the manner of graduation along the specific or specified variables, and therefore, identification of the properties could be precisely designated by the class characteristics that they bear. In accordance with this, we can have the real worth of words, syllables, letters, experience, imagination and thought in terms of the class-specific properties implanted by the species in which they occur, and, simultaneously, the effect of communication necessitated by the compliance of a category with the form in which it is situated. The idea of correlation, resolution, correspondence and transformation that is obviously intended would form the parts of the next state of the growth of a category and intended state of meaning. The constancy of correspondence, regularity of evolution, similarity of transformation would be the real events of refinement of ideational and the emotive form. In Saussurian terms every position occupied by the words, letters, syllables, sentences would be the position that has the freedom of synthesis. The prolongation of an effect so constituted will be necessarily an

---

46. Synthesis is essentially a virtue, and therefore, the resolution of transformation. In the order of evolution, it must acquire its place and position. For further description on the subject, see Ānandavardhana:

प्रसन्नगम्भीरपदा: काव्यबन्धा: सुखावहा:।
ये च तेषु प्रकारोऽयमेव योज्य: सुमेधसा।। – 3.35

addition to the system and conjugation developed earlier. The word has the power to confirm the purpose as well as the object of reason that is to be communicated to the corresponding emotive forms appropriate for the sake of wholesome advancement of the content in artistry. The question that might be asked in regard to this could be — how the inter-segmental and inter-associational framework upheld by the word could also be the basis of the act of signification approved as a measure of determining the generative content of any form? Saussure's position in this regard is one that moves over the preferential recording of the denotative intent contained in the word and its exposition to the immediately available external form. The correspondence so arrived will show an extensive medium for adjusting, readjusting, figuring and configuring, associating and resuscitating the whole situation. In accordance with the actual intention, brought about in appropriating a word for signification, the principality of formulation is at once rendered relevant as object of the word is to promote an urgency of addition in which conduct of substance and the idea will be obtained by dispersion of every single letter in the reasonable environment. The condition of comprehension beaten in Saussurian thesis would be thoroughly commuted in Roland Barthes examination of the situation. For Barthes the linguistic content (word, letter, and syllable) and emotive figure (experience, imagination, thought and the like) contained only primary specifications for the process of synthesis. Thus relationship between word and experience would be created or destroyed on the basis of the achievement of totality as a purpose by these two categories. Total completion of relative figures of value in such a way that the figure and value are real and authentic in the given sense of the medium and the context, would create the universal situations. This adds to the development of the interpretation categories in the structuralist tradition and allows us to conclude by saying that emergence of primitive relation and the creation of mordernist association at the behest of any categories undergoing modification in the artistry will be appropriately befitting for the sake of most advanced conjunction or meaning that is to emerge as a resultant of the whole process. To illustrate the situation let us consider the following verses from Ādiparva of the *Mahābhārata*:

इदं धनुर् लक्ष्यम्, इमे च बाणाः,
श्रण्वन्तु मे भू-पतयः समेताः।
छिद्रेण् यन्त्रस्य समर्पयध्वं
लक्ष्ये शितैर् व्योम-चरैर दशार्धैः।।

एतद् महत् कर्म करोति यो वै,
कुलेन रूपेण बलेन युक्तः।
तस्याद्य भार्या भगिनी ममेयं
कृष्णा भवित्री, न मृषा ब्रवीमि।। – 1.28, 29

idaṁ dhanur lakṣyam, ime ca bāṇāḥ,
śraṇvantu me bhū-patayaḥ sametāḥ ।
chidreṇ yantrasya samarpayadhvaṁ
lakṣye śitair vyoma-caraira daśārdhaiḥ ।।

etad mahat karma karoti yo vai,
kulena rūpeṇa balena yuktaḥ ।
tasyādya bhāryā bhaginī mameyaṁ
kṛṣṇā bhavitrī, na mṛṣā bravīmi ।।

In the events presented by the situations occasioned in the *Mahābhārata* we can understand that the growth of signifiers and the position of sign and consequently the magnitude of signified corresponds to the equally high growth in the constitution of substance and idea contained in the same. Every utterance is forthrightly an act of the advancement of communication, therefore, every graduation along the semantic and morphological principles is imminently virtuous.

For the same reason, one can consider how the utterances of Dhṛṣṭadyumna could confirm the process of selection and combination of those signifiers which put forth a corollary to the communication. Thus in "इदं धनुर, लक्ष्यम्, इमे च बाणाः, श्रण्वन्तु मे भू-पतयः समेताः" the purpose of progression is immediately stated and now the object is identified. इदं धनुर लक्ष्यम् indicates a prospect of time and place and, therefore, the further qualification इमे च बाणाः objectifies the content and brings it to the level of resolution. The forthcoming utterances intending the object of reason to comfortably situate the object and subject in a directional situation and therefore "छिद्रेण यन्त्रस्य समर्पयध्वं लक्ष्ये शितैर व्योम-चरैर् दशार्धैः" the process of signification is almost entirely complete. What is important to be recognised is that the description of the object and specification of the subject correspond in terms of the value to the generated figures. With this particular end in view इदं धनुर, लक्ष्यम्, इमे च बाणाः seems to be very important inasmuch as the theoretical system of communication is utilised with greater worth and relevance in that the designation, identification, proposition and the correlation of medium, content and context is accommodated with respect to the degree of refinement inscribed in each. One of the important facts related to structuralism is that it leads to emotive and linguistic configuration as a mark of an intending consciousness, therefore, the relevance of experience and adequacy of language not only present but also summarise as well.[47] The largeness of factual artistry, as we could understand from the foregoing contents in *Uttararāmacaritam*, is the intention and modification in terms of the acquisition of experiential models and linguistic categories that advance the

---

47. The linguistic models in corresponding emotive categories obtain the greatest possible reality in that every word, letter syllable, sentence, *bhāva*, *vibhāva*, *anubhāva*, *sthāyībhāva sañcārībhāva*, thought, and experience is situated on the explication of the concentrated value for itself. For further description on the subject, see Ānandavardhana and Saussure.

progression till the time point of interception is arrived at. In other words, the models of configuration realistically intervene and uphold the structural formation until the progress of synthesis is actually complete.

The manner of obtaining signification could be either by distorting or by mutating the signifiers. The distortion of signifiers invents a process of synchrony, while mutation will affect a manner of diachrony, yet in either of the situations, the strength of the effect would be different. For example, look at the Sabhāparva of *Mahābhārata*:

> एतच्छ्रुत्वा व्यवसितां, निकृतिं समुपाश्रितः।
> "जितं" इत्येव शकुनिर् युधिष्ठिरं अभाषत ।। – 79

> *etacchrutvā vyavasitāṁ, nikṛtiṁ samupāśritaḥ* ।
> *"jitaṁ" ityeva śakunir yudhiṣṭhiraṁ abhāṣata* ।।

Here we can understand how the act of presentation and the manner of reception is facilitated by the margins of progression. On the other hand, the relationship between addresser and addressee is compounded with generic marks of succession. At the beginning the figure is invented in terms of reference in which victory at the gambling by Kauravas is announced forthwith by Śakuni almost without any truth in it. And Yudhiṣṭhira having never had the occasion of telling or listening to any lie whatsoever, accepted it as being true and consequently gave away everything that he had at his command. In this situation the creation of an order of communication through designated signs is the mark of the strength. Addresser's identification and transformation into an addressee or vice versa is brought about by the cumulation of inverted correspondence and thus in each of the acts of progression of addresser towards addressee, the events of communication have themselves become the fully developed meaning for the sake of interpretation and comprehension of the whole circumstances. Śakuni intends and obtains graduation of the communicative process by both adding an effect of surprise to intensly morphological process. Thus when he says "जितं" he inverts the contents and expands the natural position of dissociation and correlation. For this reason we could understand how projected appearance is also the condition of felt reality, and, in fact, the imminence of the structuralist form is understood.

In *dhvani* system, the intention of kind, quality, manner and terms of transformation are situated in the fact of correlation and association that are understood to be both upward and downward; vertical and horizontal in the shape, sign and effect. This particular emphasis enhances the prospects of growth of primary, secondary and tertiary forms of an artistic situation. One of the achievements of Ānandavardhana is that he has developed the extent of semiotic, phonological, morphological, semantic and syntactical figures appropriately as it should be universally presented. In each, the native circumstance seems to be exactly proportional for the sake of the development of an exclusive principal form. The nature of any linguistic category is to develop medium-oriented specification, so much so, that the propagation of content, of necessity, would involve the revival of every preceding and succeeding coordinate. It would further mean that the strength of category is located in advancement of the medium. Taking this as a precept, Ānandavardhana develops the conceptual form of absolute, total, aggregate, concentrated universal in order that a category may enter into the locale of reason and cognition. Thus the idea is not only excellent but also worthwhile for the creation of totality as a process of continuity for the sake of an achievement of proportion and balance, both as a measure of commitment and participation. The acquisition of this condition is creative of assertive forms in the general structure of the category. The linguistic constructs like *śabda* and *pada* propose an order of rationality by reconstructing the crude inferences drawn from the emotive categories like, *bhāva, vibhāva,* etc. and confer an order of synthesis by amalgamating the differences between point of perception and the condition of recreation.[48] The event of finding an exact value of interpretation so as to promote an urgency of absolute could be seen to be as important development suggested by Ānandavardhana in the area of enrichment. In fact, the elevation in *śabda* from the status of an individualised and isolated category to the height of compound category holding up the terms of synthesis by opposition and difference is also what could be presented as an aspect of the whole situation.

In *dhvani* and the structuralist poetics, the origin of totality in terms of inception and advancement could be seen to be broadly responding to the idea of strength and potential of the contents, variables, coordinates and locations of the participating categories and the constructs. For this reason, expansion of *bhāva, vibhāva, śabda, pada* on the one hand and language, thought, imagination and experience on the other is in fact conceived by appropriation, ordering, regulation, conjunction, addition, multiplication of the content and medium involved in each. It is, thus, with this groundwork scheme of evolution of the categories for the sake of an ideal artistry is proposed.

Constitution of the text in consequence of the achievement of resolution of an object into event is supposed to be

---

48. *Śabda* has to be an effect of gradual expansion in which substance, identity, motif, purpose and relation are always added. Pāṇini would suggest that growth of a word is necessarily both, vertical and horizontal. Therefore it anticipates a complete formation. For further description on the subject, see Pāṇini: समर्थानां प्रथमाद्वा (1.82).

synonymous with the creation of wholeness in the artistic circumstances via the enrichment and the expansion of the categories participating in the creation of an ideal artistry in *dhvani*. The origin of the categories like *śabda, pada, bhāva, vibhāva, anubhāva, sthāyībhāva, sañcārībhāva, ālambana* and *uddīpana* is associated with the progressive development of the artistic situation as a totally absolute formation and in that way the enrichment of every category is, itself, of consequence.[49] For that matter, the beginning of the event of association also marks an end of the situation leading to the formation method, appropriate measures, direct reasolution and concrete assimilation. The advancement of content to ensure habituated perception just for the sake of the renewal of correspondence and correlation would be further added to by the imminence of purpose for the sake of final modification. As the terms suggestive of the idea of *dhvani* are befitting, even when the time sequence and the time event both are adopted for accommodation and adjusted against one another. Ānandavardhana conveniently suggests the point that there can be a major and appreciable difference between the cause and effect of the time and virtual determinant of the situation. In other words, every event of time is to be designated as appropriate to specify the formulation of the organic whole. The idea of whole is commensurate with the optimum precision and refinement suggested by the growth of modified perspective in the category, and, therefore, from beginning till end *bhāva, pada, vibhāva,* and *anubhāva* obtain

---

49. The conventions and traditions that have brought the word to its present formative significance plays an important part in bringing about *dhvani*. Patañjali in the *Mahābhāṣa* makes it pertinent that final resolution in terms of the meaning is a procedure that is born and invented through a series of preceding systematisation woven into the organic cycle of the language. For further description on the subject, see Patañjali: लोकतोऽर्थप्रयुक्ते शब्दप्रयोगे शास्त्रेण् धर्मनियमः (1.1).

magnitude and strength to satisfy the imminence of artistic possibility, hence the modification is complete and universal. For example, we may think of the following verses of Baudelaire in "Flowers of Evil":

> Soon cold shadows will close over us
> and summer's transitory gold be gone;
> near them chopping firewood in our Court
> the dreary thud of logs on cobblestone.
> Winter will come to repossess my soul
> With rage and outrage, horror, drudgery,
> and like the Sun in its polar holocaust
> my heart will be a block of blood — red ice.
> I listen trembling to that grim tattoo —
> build a gallows it would sound the same.
> My mind becomes a tower giving way
> under the impact of a battering — ram.
> Stunned by the stocks, I seem to hear, somewhere,
> a coffin hurridly hammered shut — for whom?
> Summer was yesterday; autumn is here!
> Strange how that sound rings out like a farewell. — 1-16

In these verses, Baudelaire conceives the idea of unchangeability of the basic circumstances of life, therefore, he introduces us to a situation in which the necessity of communication with the nature as an event is lost. What, in fact, is happening is that the poet understands that the time will keep changing but the good time the poet had will perhaps never come back to him. Accordingly, he isolates himself and thus resigns himself to seclusion where brooding and meditation for the sake of the life speculation could be brought forth. For the matter of that, he finds cold, winter and autumn to be duplicating, replicating and multiplying themselves so as to generate the necessity of order, function, precision and goodness in life. Yet for the poet it would only be the same suffering, same sorrow and similar sets of confusion brought about.

Looking at the poet from the perspectives of *dhvani* poetics, we could understand that the opening itself is creative of an order or sequence (क्रम) and for that same reason the principal emotion (लक्ष्य) of the situation is defined. At the beginning poet speaks of *"soon cold shadow will close over us"* and at once implants the possibility of growth and development of the artistic situation, *cold shadow* brings about a series of generative units in that it invites observer's patience in waiting for the next turn of the time, hence summer's transitory gold issues in a direct consequence and in turn the idea of summer being pleasant builds up the necessity of having another set of time in the form of winter. To complete the idea of winter being the harbinger of *rage* and *outrage, horror* and *drudgery* finally gives way to the eternal suffering of the poet, and, of necessity, would mean that for him there is no escape from the perennial sorrow described in a *"coffin" "hurridly hammered shut"*. For him it would only be the change in the external world inasmuch as *"summar was yesterday" "autumn is here"* . . . *"rings out like a farewell"*.

The substantial position occupied by the words and experience would themselves speak of the extraordinarily rich position of each. In consequence *cold shadows* invents summer's transitory golds implicated in the next analysis in winter and finally terminates into autumn. Naturally, the words are chronologically placed in a sequence (क्रम) while each word extends the idea of correlation only by being suggested at the tertiary level. Besides, the words instruct a proposition for the sake of the metaphor. In fact, metaphor obtained in "cold shadows", "polar holocaust", "battering-raw", "coffin" and the like would certainly advance the notion that there is an exceptional charm, lucidity, force, strength, hidden in these words. Because of this, there is also the situation of evolution for that matter "cold shadows" finally evolves into a *"coffin"*, *"horridly hammered shut"*. By the standard of experience, the comprehensibility in strength of the underlying *bhāvas* may also be substantially explicated. The passage, on the whole, is expression of *karuṇa* yet however, the traces of *bībhatsa* are at once imminent and similarly to this account the conduct of all the experience is towards an addition to strength of *karuṇa*. It would mean that the order of growth of artistry is precisely outlined. Looking at the existing situation, it would definitely possible to say that words and experience both enter into the state of expansion through replacement and reinvention and finally lead to the strength of universal artistry. For the similar reasons an ideal groundwork for the emergence of *dhvani* system is understood. Similarly, in the structuralist situation the fully grown text could be considered to be the product of the addition of the finally evolved sign, signifier and signified. In the next place, it would mean that the possibility of having a letter, syllable, word and sentence along with the corresponding experience should direct the insistence on upgradation, elevation and refinement so much so that every instance of the word (for that matter every single letter and syllable) could inculcate the highest framework of universal significance and condition. The existence of reality as one of the necessary conditions of meaning is something that could be termed as the idea of text. Saussure states:

> But the statement that everything in language is negative is true only if the signified and the signifier are considered separately; when we consider the sign in its totality we have something that is positive in its own class. A linguistic system is a series of differences of sound combined with a series of differences of ideas; but the pairing of a certain number of acoustical signs with as many cuts made from the mass of thought engenders a system of values; and this system serves as the effective link between the phonic and psychological elements within each sign. Although both the signified and the signifier are purely differential and negative when considered separately, their combination is

> a positive fact; it is even the sole type of facts that language has, for maintaining the parallelism between the two classes of differences, is the distinctive function of the linguistic institution. —121

In Saussure's opinion, the procedure of enrichment and refinement must circumstantially be evident as a part of the effort to bring together several units and several parts. In the first place, it has to be remembered that the limit of a sign is not contained in any distinction that might be arrived at between corresponding sound image and subsequent formation of the value. The progress of sign is, in fact, concentration of maturity of the continuity between the expectations and reality of value-added projection. For this reason, the property of a word/letter/syllable could always be fundamentally generative of equivalence in which interrelation and extra-relation; proto-relation and Propter-relation could be at once observed. This would confirm the fact that existence of two identical signs at any point of time in any ideal linguistic situation is expected to bring about an immediate injunction so much so that the method of sound image and the magnitude of concept could be well understood. Saussurian position doesn't exclude the fact that the advancement of sign could not successfully be the realistic inculcation of a certified value. In fact, in every instance in which the location of determinate sign is possible, the concepts will equally conjugate by the laws of combination. The next important situation with which Saussure deals with is the state of forming a conduct with regard to explication of the signs. There can be two different ways to explain the wholesome idea inherent upon a progressing sign. There is the certainty of fixing up a value in the immediacy of the events, moreover, the arbitrariness is relatively insignificant when the term of value approaches the facts of sound configuration. In fact, the idea of holding up immutable or mutable sign could be conferred, as a rule, on the principle that the beginning of a word as a source of possible sound function is primary, yet, while it reaches a state of prolongation the content forms are lengthened and therefore it becomes secondary, significant and meaning oriented. The nature of text that we are trying to infuse into the situation is the best available equivalent of disposable, distributed terms of the sign function in which every consequence of concept is inscribed wilfully in the canonical sequence propagated and developed for the purpose. Text, therefore, must function in accordance with the extraction and refraction of the progression of concentrated content variable. In forming a consortium of interdependent and formatively secure sequence of the linguistic contents, we become able to harmonise even the remotest and practically insignificant aspects of the sign. In the following verses of Śūdraka's *Mṛcchakaṭikam*, the appropriation and selection of the intensity of commuted sign constituting a formulation for whole system could be seen and understood:

स्खलति चरणं भूमौ न्यस्तं न चार्द्रतमा मही,
स्फुरति नयनं वामो बाहुर्मुहुश्च विकम्पते।
शकुनिरपरश्चायं तावद्विरोति हि नैकशः,
कथयति महाघोरं मृत्युं न चात्र विचारणा।। – 2.13

skhalati caraṇaṁ bhūmau nyastaṁ na cārdratamā mahī,
sphurati nayanaṁ vāmo bāhurmuhuśca vikampate।

śakuniraparaścāyaṁ tāvadviroti hi naikaśaḥ,
kathayati mahāghoraṁ mṛtyuṁ na cātra vicāraṇā।।

Here the conviction that something ominous is about to happen develops the attendant notion of object-intention and subject-function. Subject of the verses is the inconstancy of appearance and thus the character falls upon aberration both in perception and thought. He disapproves the idea that there would be a meeting with the beloved rather he considers the prospect of rejection. In this way union with the beloved and separation from the beloved have found worthy objects for expression and communication. The proposition developed through sign could be held out to be generally significant. The moving (trembling) body and the stationary earth suggest the ethics of opposition and difference, while bursting/robbing/ bulging/protruding and the deflection of the left arm occasioned by the chirping of the birds introduce another set of correlatives to extend the function of signifiers. It could be seen that basic preoccupation is to suggest that there is the impossibility in being united with the beloved. Accordingly, the stationary earth is brought against the movement of different forms and events contained in the "arm", "bird" and the "eye" and ultimately the signified that emerges is inevitable progress towards the death. What is important to understand is that the hierarchy of signifiers has a graduation along the introduction of the effect of wonder and surprise, or, at that, the astonishment and shock. Every movement calculates a precision at the amalgamation of revelation of the fact that what is hidden in the midst of unworthy movements observed in the eye, the arm, and the birds assuages the feeling of having an unexpected meeting as that is also an uncertainty. In this situation, the coordination of sign is culturally and historically antecedental to the reality of actual object. Thus the assemblage of a curious inventory for the sake of romance speaks of the high cultural values assigning both rule and function to women in the remote antiquity of Indian cultural tradition. The eye bulges just to advance the notion that the hidden conviction of being in love is not at all certified in any union whatsoever. Thus the subject only prospers at the will of the fancy. This, therefore, is an attitude that would govern the formal arrangement and in the last analysis would generate a variety of signs intended in the eye, the bird and the arm. It is also a matter of investigation that organic units (eye, birds, and arm) lead to the creation of an organic whole (the complete body). In other words the dominant male function regulated through gestural projection for inviting the female to be united both as an aspect of physical and material signification. Sensory intention in that way finds an application in the material projection of the situation, yet the scheme to be understood is only the fact that opposition between male and female is the source of perennial change.

The textuality of linguistic and experiential methods adopted for the sake of harmonious creation is worth examination, and, to this end we find that the entire system is based on expository and additive signifiers inasmuch as one typical function of human body adopts itself to circumlocate both conventional and modernist methods of male/female dichotomy. The beginning of the entire theme on this note successfully affirms the progressive form and almost like the progressing waves in which every preceding semi-circle is transmuted into succeeding and forthcoming significance. The adjustment of signifiers along the committed margins and inculcation of signified at a point at which the concept and image both meet, could be understood to be as the germinal situation and it is also important to note that displacement of suggesting movement and in turn presupposing transmutation is the mark of concrete situation developed in the text. Every sign for that matter offers an intention to complete the act of conjugation. For example स्खलति in this, conveys the sense of being desperate and deviated into uncertainty and the idea is carried further by obtaining similarity in contention. Consequently स्फुरति and बाहुर्मुहुश्च, नैकशः and महाघोरं मृत्युं could build up lengthened contention to prove the point that aberration in (uncertainty and impossibility) organic function of instinct could bring about direct signification. With this intention, the poet combines variance with association and thus each act of displacement is in itself a further mark of assertion in terms of concept projection. There can be substantial series of interrelational facts and the observation of स्खलति is primarily a necessary step in presenting right perspective of the complete structure. The important aspect that has been noticed in the foregoing stanza is that the structuralist situation proposes an assertion. The determinate necessity of figural as well as formal constitution of every single act of expression, and for this reason, every single unit of linguistic and experiential constitution is seen as forming completely active form. Consequently phonological, morphological, semantic and semiotic units cohere and present poise and balance with regard to correspondence, assimilation, correlation cognition and effective transmutation into each other. The act of reference as a part of massive resurgence of correlatives becomes the part of meaning constitution. It would now be easier, looking at the perspective developed in the above statement, to validate the structuralist identification of text as being a substance whose formative exposition is validated or concretised through interconvertible relations existing amongst certain basic features identified in sound, meaning, grammar, words and the sign forms. Such a plan of organisation leads to an authentic proposition, which we can conveniently term as text. The property of addition, and similarly, reduction, are the two important characteristics accommodated to an effect in the prolongation of the underlying units and parts. The genuine version of the text takes into consideration every possibility of successful resolution and obtains the following characteristics:

1. It is built around facts developed by the selection and identification of concrete terms in opposition to the abstract terms.

2. The generative units present a hierarchy in that there is a direct division of immediately expressive term into orthodox universal term. For this reason the relation between phonological, morphological, syntactical,

semantic and semiotic content is always synchronised one after another.

3. The effect of one content forming unit (phonological, morphological, etc.) is precisely to square the resultant benefit out of continuous accumulation of meaning-oriented forms around it.
4. The unit developed for the purpose opts for exclusion of weaker semantic contents in the ideal transformation, is possible only amongst the selection of higher forms.
5. The units of the participating categories compete with the necessarily redundant signifiers, and, on that account, bring about an expressive system of conformity.

The event of formation of text as a form is the most comprehensive interaction between the uncalculable effect of organisation and presentative fact of communication. The period in which the linguistic unit and the experiential categories come to have the meaning and significance is also at the same time an appropriate description of the universal system of figures, forms, codes, ethics and the like. Thus, in the structuralist terms, text is an occupant of significance and the synthesis brought about by interactive transformation of linguistic and experiential categories. The appropriation of textual universality as envisaged and comprehended in *dhvani* and structuralist poetics ultimately takes up two basic issues for the sake of constitution and explication. In the first place, the formal ethics implanted in the reader and secondly the authentic and unified whole of units and parts called the text as such, is incorporated into a network of relations and interrelations and each is defined in terms of propriety of meaning equivalence of content, adequacy of medium and the like. It is to be understood that the upgradation and succession of the content in *dhvani* system brings about extremely precise order of presentation, and, therefore, the coordination of categories and the equivalence of the contents, both are significantly directly proportional to each other.[50] Because of this reason, it is possible to observe the chronology of absolutes thoroughly distributed along the proximal and distal ends of the creative situation. The text that thereby comes up in sequence, therefore, carries the characteristics of presentation and exposition, and, thus, communicates to the reader with great success. In fact, the altering inversion, codification and harmonisation could be seen to be the various stages through which the effect of experience and suggestivity of the language openly approve for the sake of realisation by the reader. The definition of text in *dhvani* is precisely one that is suggestive of thoroughgoing ideational conjunction in which every conjunction is perfectly an absolute on its own. Ānandavardhana in *Dhvanyāloka* makes mention of the fact in the following manner:

प्रसन्नगम्भीरपदाः काव्यबन्धाः सुखावहाः।
ये च तेषु प्रकारोऽयमेव यौज्यः सुमेधसा।।

वाच्यालङ्कारवर्गोऽयं व्यङ्ग्यांशानुगमें सति।
प्रायेणैव परां छायां विभ्रल्लक्ष्ये निरीक्ष्यते।। – 3.35, 36

prasannagambhīrapadāḥ kāvyabandhāḥ sukhāvahāḥ ।
ye ca teṣu prakāro 'yameva yaujyaḥ sumedhasā ।।

vācyālaṅkāravargo 'yaṁ vyaṅgayāṁśānugameṁ sati ।
prāyeṇaiva parāṁ chāyāṁ vibhrallakṣye nirīkṣyate ।।

---

50. In *dhvani* the invention of significance as a part of creation of total effect would be held to be the greatest contribution inasmuch as creation of meaning is concerned. For further description on the subject, see Bhartṛhari:

अनादिनिधनं ब्रह्म शब्दतत्त्वं यदक्षरम्।
विवर्ततेऽर्थभावेन प्रक्रिया जगतो यतः।। – 1

We can understand from this that the availability of actually precise categories and the poet's own competence in utilising them for the sake of development of an aggregate form, that he should like to inculcate, would enjoin upon a resultant comprehensibility that he will inculcate and induct to constitute the universal structure in which every content will approximately render the effect of continuous universality, continuous restructuring, strengthen, generative universality; and these would contain the real meanings of the system that we would like to call text. In these circumstances, the characteristics will obviously befit the meaning of the event and therefore, cognition, exposition presentation and resolution will be the major coordinates of artistic competence. Even otherwise, in the structuralist tradition, the imminence of rigid, steadfast, pure, organic and continuous evocation of content detail, medium, data and context interpretation, situate the acceptability of text as an agency of resolution for the sake of the purity of reader. In this, the larger forms of communication presupposing equivalence between homogeneous and heterogeneous aspects of artistry are supposedly brought about. It is thus, the efficiency of an event in which the whole structure of the categories comes to present itself for the sake of assured changes into the absolute in which reliability of text as an authority of signification is implied.

2

Formal Methods II
Resolution and Convergence of the Categories

THE presentation of an effect of the artistry and exposition of the magnitude of transformation and resolution would invariably suggest a significance of the characteristics of function and inscription of the absolute right from the beginning and till the end. While it must be admitted that cross-cultural application of the theories violates ethical and moral grounds on which a work of art is supposed to be thriving, yet, however, the unquestionable autonomy enjoyed by the functional categories and assorted contexts would go a long way to constitute proportion, synthesis and an equilibrium so necessary for the perpetuation of artistic varieties and standards. It is of no significance, however, that the creativity is, out of necessity, a production of precise cultural focus, hence, it is more inclined towards socio-religious and religio-historical situations. In putting up an application of theories on the texts that have become canonical and yet belong to different cultures and religious set-ups, from the theory that is to be applied. In the following pages, we have made on attempt to generate a law of concentrated equilibrium of the artistic situation through which we purport to indicate the existence of suitable, commonplace, exact, truthful, real, actual and obvious correlatives for the achievement of functionality within and outside, and beyond and below the artistic situation. In *dhvani* and the structuralist poetics, the intention to promote the convergence and synthesis of the artistry is obviously the greatest because of the basic constitution of the categories, constructs and models operative upon the whole system. In fact, the initiation that is undertaken to reform and reconstruct the primordial condition of artistry happens to be an important part of the emphasis that is laid on the procedure of the building up an adequate degree of strength. It must be admitted as a rule that rationalised experience and ratiocinated language bring together the essence of formative adequacy. In reality, as Ānandavardhana would like to suggest, the process of evolution of language into an ideal experience, and an ideal experience into language, would continue till the absolute forms are at once imminent. As a measure to prevent the ideal language and ideal experience from any decay, by the virtue of loss in addition or subtraction of functional and positive contents or context or medium, Ānandavardhana should like to suggest the pre-imminence of a single authoritative instrument of reception and transformation. In other words, every content, construct and medium due upon the language and experience must reinvent themselves through a single and composite universal methodology of figuration. This would enforce the act of transformation that would suit the ethics of configuration of genuine artistic situation. In the structuralist poetics, the model of perception records an implicit concomitance of realisation in that morphological, semantic, phonological, syntactical and semiotic structures obtain the thoroughgoing position and representation with regard to an effective change and transformation of their immediate form into the canonical universals. This adds to the emphasis that Saussure lays on an understanding of given linguistic facts in relation to its wholesome growth or evolution through the time.

Immediately, one understands how the propositional certainty brings together various seminal structures like metaphor, metanomy and the like. The urgency of such an act to invent homogeneous medium, so as to raise concrete structures for the emergence of meaning, could ultimately be due upon the transmuted versions of structures and their progression. For this reason, transference and communication would ideally seem to be two composite standards for the reinvention of total meaning. These characteristics would ultimately suggest the possibility of finding the configuration of meaning obtained on account of the precision created in the foregoing modes of the structures. This, therefore, would be the paradigm to find out the methods of application of structuralism on the Indian texts and for that matter of *dhvani* and the Western texts.

Structuralist poetics is based on the law of generation, and accordingly, it offers to understand the comprehensibility of primary structures of the linguistic formulation and also the linguistic structure of an experiential model especially when an artistic situation is underlying. By structure, obviously Saussure, Barthes, Jakobson and others would mean how the concept of a system could associate itself with the changes that the context, content medium would impose on the evolving situation. Evolution is a necessity to understand how and why any structure (phonological, morphological, semantic, semiotic, or syntactical) originates and undergoes changes through the designated historical periods, and, during this course, either becomes an addition to something else or acquires the addition of something else. It might also be possible that graphological or phonetic form, either in totality or in parts, may be lost or subtracted from it. In either of the cases, there is a change of the form, yet however, meaning composes an order and existence of any linguistic or experiential category. The following terms would therefore befit the forthcoming logic of application — (1) structural apparatus configures exact and total units and parts of the categories (2) in an artistic situation worth of phonology, morphology, semantic, semeiotic, syntactics is wholesome (3) metaphor is an instrument of transformation, (4) emergence of an ideal meaning is conceived through evolution of the figures which could be either linguistics on experiential, (5) there is a correspondence of a total structure (identified through meaning or value) with the prevailing cultural system, therefore, the upgraded metaphor operating in the form of myths may also be included into the curriculum of structuralist interpretation.

The first important scriptural epic we should like to take into consideration is the *Mahābhārata*. In the *Mahābhārata*, the battle between good and evil has been presented on the universal scale, so much so that it preoccupies itself with the creation and destruction in the universe, hence naturally, gods also are the benefactors of the situation. The Pāṇḍavas who uphold the reign of virtue have lost their empire and Kauravas' embodying evil are now mounting the glory and victory. The forthcoming events precisely deal with the benediction accorded to virtue, hence to Pāṇḍavas, and the resultant curse that befalls on Kauravas.

To comprehend the situation as a rich occasion for analysis one could state that meaning-oriented and meaning forming structures are evolving continuously all along this scriptural epic. Consider, for example, Swayaṁvaraparva of the *Mahābhārata* of Veda Vyāsa:

गत्वा तु तां भार्गवकर्मशालां
पार्थौ पृथां प्राप्य महानुभावौ।
तां याज्ञसेनीं परमप्रतीतौ
भिक्षेत्ययावेदयतां नराग्र्यौ।।

कुटीगता सा त्वनवेक्ष्य पुत्रौ
प्रोवाच भुङ्क्तेति समेप्य सर्वे।

पश्चध कुन्ती प्रसमीक्ष्यकृष्णां
कष्टं भया भाषितमित्युवाच।। – 1, 2

gatvā tu tāṁ bhārgavakarmaśālāṁ
pārtho pṛthāṁ prāpya mahānubhāvau।
tāṁ yājñasenīṁ pramapratītau
bhikṣetyayāvedayatāṁ narāgyau।।

kuṭīgatā sā tvanavekṣya putrau
provāca bhuṅkteti samepya serve।
paścadha kuntī prasmīkṣyakṛṣṇāṁ
kaṣṭaṁ bhayā bhāṣitamityuvāca।।

In this passage, the presentation of an inquisition and reception of the same inquisition are stretched, elongated and expanded to the extent of realisable material formation, therefore, what appears to be infinite is in fact a calculable reality. At the beginning, when Bhīma and Arjuna let their mother know about the offerings they got while begging all around and the reply they got from the mother for equitable distribution amongst them was, in fact, an exercise that raised the metaphorical principle of semantic inversion. Inquisition is operating through the inversion of appropriate sign and thus every word carries the necessity of communication inasmuch as the inquisition offers variety of semantic indices graduated in the order of rising intensity. In the whole structure, the order of the words and the scale in which the words are graduated for the sake of transformation, is very important inasmuch as group of words select and expose a condition of sign to the acquisition of preferred value. गत्वा तु तां भार्गवकर्मशालां and it would be easily understood that the meaning is accumulated through an act of reorganisation hence immediately it is followed by पार्थो पृथां प्राप्य महानुभावौ. It follows from this that object as a modifier achieves its modification in the universal form that is being invented. For this reason the two signs compliment each other. Investing the word (lexicons) with inverted signification is also a mark of excellence of the passage. Every word infuses into a rhetorical question and therefore congregates maximum effects through resolving the whole situation into communicable signifiers. Accordingly, भार्गवकर्मशालां, भिक्षेत्ययावेदयतां, भुङ्क्तेति, समेत्य सर्वे confer value orientation on the whole situation. It is worth mentioning that the effect is composite and therefore the growth of signifier would be seen to be arranged in a proper sequence. The characteristic effect that is obtained in the continuation of such a metamorphosis is the exchange of metaphor through mutated signifier; for example पार्थो पृथां प्राप्य महानुभावौ and प्रोवाच भुङ्क्तेति समेप्य सर्वे could intentionally form a mechanism of exchange of adding properties inasmuch as what is being brought as alms must now be distributed amongst all the recipients. This would add to the meaning that object and subject both are having complimentary formation पार्थो पृथां acquires and invents a motif of transference in समेत्य सर्वे. Similarly, the other words like प्राप्य and सर्वे commute themselves to formalise a synthesis to the external that unit has now become the part or the part in other words is now the whole. In fact, it is better to say that semantic, morphological and syntactic and even semiotic units first disperse themselves along the random distribution, hence it begins with गत्वा तु तां and continues through पार्थो पृथां, तां याज्ञसेनीं, भिक्षेत्ययावेदयतां, त्वनवेक्ष्य पुत्रौ प्रसमीक्ष्यकृष्णां. Yet everything culminates into समेप्य सर्वे. What is important here is, the equitable distribution of primary units of signifiers and consolidated evolution of the secondary units of signification and the creation of universals at the tertiary stage of the growth. We can perhaps better understand the entire framework by remodelling the situation along the following graphics:

Primary signifiers — भार्गव कर्मशालां, याज्ञसेनीं परमप्रतीतौ भिक्षेत्ययावेदयतां, कुटीगता, त्वनवेक्ष्य पुत्रौ प्रसमीक्ष्यकृष्णां

Secondary significatory unit — प्रोवाच भुङ्क्तेति

Tertiary universals — समेत्य सर्वे

The actual circumstance of creation of the structure of meaning and the structure of value could be seen to be having the direct effect of modification. What actually happens is that the contents acquire specific order of progression and the term of progression may be linear or cyclical. In either of the circumstances, context and medium both are enriched with the nearest and also the largest association with equivalent forms. Enhancement of the ability to acquire newer models of concept is basically the property that is based on the form of immediate association acquired on account of evolution through primary morphological and phonetic objects. In the above illustration, we can understand that how भार्गवकर्मशालां initiates an action upon association that finally enlists more strengthened conjugation of concrete variants, and thus, we can understand how भुङ्क्तेति समेप्य सर्वे performs mutation of empirical function of enrichment. What finally emerges is the precision and the universality of the effect inscribed in कष्ट भया भाषितमित्युवाच.

In the forthcoming episodes of the *Mahābhārata*, the crisis that has come up in consequence of Draupadī having been obtained as alms and also having been laid by the mother to be equally distributed among the five brothers (in the sheer presumption of something being of solid and material import). The situation, now, stands qualified to the manner of interpretation we are proposing. The Pāṇḍavas are the models of the urgency of communication and among the five Yudhiṣṭhira is supposed to conduct the transfer of an experience to the other models. Draupadī, on the other hand, is an object from which the signifiers must originate and therefore also present themselves for the signifiers. It must now come to our comprehension that combination and selection both are eminently fixing up the evolving metaphor towards the total and final effect. For example, look at Ādiparva of the *Mahābhārata* of Veda Vyāsa:

इयं तु कन्या द्रुपदस्य राज्ञः
तवानुजाभ्यां मयि संनिविष्टा।
यथोचितं पुत्र मयापि चोक्तं
समेत्य भुङ्क्षेति नृप प्रभादात्।।

मया कथं नानृतमुक्तभद्य
भवेत करुणमृषभ् ब्रवीहि।
पाञ्चालराजस्य सुतामधर्मो
न चोपवर्तेत न विभ्रमेच्च ।। – 4, 5

iyaṁ tu kanyā drupadasya rājñaḥ
tavānujābhyāṁ mayi saṁniviṣṭā ।
yathocitaṁ putra mayāpi coktaṁ
sametya bhuṅkteti nṛpa prabhādāt ।।

mayā kathaṁ nānṛtamuktabhadya
bhaveta karuṇamṛṣabh bravīhi ।
pāñcālarājasya sutāmadharmo
na copavarteta na vibhramecca ।।

Now it would be quite logical to maintain that affirmative and negative occasions of conjunctions open up a series of value-oriented structures in the present context where ignorance seems to be bliss inasmuch as Draupadī now is all set to become the wife to the five Pāṇḍavas. The description of the event has two important characteristics. In the first place, the semantic intention is in the process of conversion and therefore it comes through the effect of surprise. This occasions the revival and exposition of additive and associative syntax through which every instance of encoding presents the growth of signification. For this reason, the beginning, when Kuntī seems to be admitting and exhorting the intention as a consequence of generous association. Thus she says — इयं तु कन्या द्रुपदस्य राज्ञः. The morphology and syntax are commuted through the direction of evolution that they suggest. For this reason, the transformation of object corresponds to the communication of the different lexicons. It is very important to note that the signifiers that are immediately available and the signifiers, which are remotely conceived, both unify themselves across the height of developing situation. It is on account of the curiosity, wonder and surprise of Kuntī in having commanded her sons to distribute equally whatever was obtained as an alm and Pāṇḍavas in having Draupadī as their wife. The contention provided here could move the signifiers to an absolutely concrete position and every signifier ultimately conferring equilibrium to the contorted forms. Inception of wonder by extracting the centre as a model of configuration for the world could be observed in words like — इदं तु कन्या द्रुपदस्य राज्ञः and also in तवानुजाभ्यां मयि संनिविष्टा. The basic property observed in each of the syntactical units is that each procures maximum support from the medium and thus the length of configuration is substantially located in the primacy of syntax. The act of signification is basically the intention that brings forth the union of corresponding morphological segments and for this reason इयं तु कन्या and मया कथं fall upon the cyclical consequence of progression. The further developments in Swayaṁvaraparva could bring forth more interesting results with regard to the structuralist situation. For example, consider Ādiparva of the *Mahābhārata* of Veda Vyāsa:

अर्जुनवाच -
मा मां नरेन्द्र त्वमधर्मभाजं
कृथा न धर्मोऽयमशिष्टदृष्टः
भवान निवेश्य प्रथमं ततोऽयं
भीमो महाबाहुरचिन्त्यकर्मा।।

अहं ततो नकुलोऽनन्तरं मे
पश्चादयं सहदेवस्तरस्वी।

वृकोदरोऽहं च यमौ च राजन्नियं
च कन्या भवतो नियोज्यः।। – 8, 9

arjunavāca —
mā māṁ narendra tvamadharmabhājaṁ
kṛthā na dharmo 'yamaśiṣṭadṛṣṭaḥ
bhavāna niveśya prathamaṁ tato 'yaṁ
bhīmo mahābāhuracintyakarmā ।।

ahaṁ tato nakulo 'nantaraṁ me
paścādayaṁ sahadevastarasvī ।
vṛkodaro 'haṁ ca yamau ca rājanniyaṁ
ca kanyā bhavato niyojyaḥ ।।

What is important in this passage is that the synchronised syntax overlaps and inserts the active semantic proposition. For this reason, belief and disbelief; appearance and reality; truth and untruth, are all combined into one. मा मां नरेन्द्र त्वमधर्मभाजं is an activity that could be assigned to the restoration of the greatest value figures in the forthcoming parts of the verses. It is for this reason that inability to accept (भवान निवेश्य प्रथमं ततोऽयं) revives the growth of signifiers all around. Subsequently, it is to be seen that comprehensibility and the achievement of contention is really very significant. Consistency in projecting along the centre of organisation could form a sufficient basis for ascribing the excellence of the verse to the strength of craftsmanship. The request for non-admittance on the part of Arjuna is, in fact, an encoding for the sake of value that proliferates both vertically and horizontally along the whole situation. Thus the exercise of synchronised option in भीमो महाबाहुरचिन्त्यकर्मा and अहं ततो नकुलोऽनन्तरं मे and even otherwise the formalised structure of signification in पश्चादयं सहदेवस्तरस्वी. The manner in which affirmation and denial are regulated and controlled could speak of a shift in the scale of progression. Accordingly, multiplicity in having many signs ultimately mutate to the finality of one. With this particular situation at hand we can put forth an argument that, Narendra, Bhīmasena, Arjuna, Nakula, and Sahadeva each comprehends a model of signification.

The extension of structure by introducing confirmed variables is precisely the manner through which meaning is determined. One of the facts that will have to be understood is now the turn of phonetic or morphological situation that renewes the strength of association in each. For this reason the metaphor that comes up and grows along, holds the strength of meaning. For example, in Ādiparva of the *Mahābhārata* we can fix up the similar situation:

एतेषां यो धनुः श्रेष्ठ सज्यं कुर्याद, द्विजोत्तम।
तस्मै प्रदेया भगिनी, सत्यमुक्तं मया वचः॥ – 2.22

eteṣaṁ yo dhanuḥ śreṣṭha sajyaṁ kuryāda, dvijottama ।
tasmai pradeyā bhaginī, satyamuktaṁ mayā vacaḥ ॥

In this the presentation of association of universal form in धनुः श्रेष्ठ carries the total effect of meaning. धनुः श्रेष्ठ is a measure of strength through which one can revive the spirit of divinity inasmuch as धनुः embodies the divine himself. In other words, we can state the proposition by saying that the object is an effort to recreate the sense of order in this world with the authority of divine looming large in the background. The facts of metaphor are stated in the improvisation and consolidation of the sign and signifiers and interestingly each is paradigmatic in nature. धनुः श्रेष्ठ envisages both the cause and effect, thus explicates associative variants in सज्यं, द्विजोत्तम, सत्यमुक्तं and वचः. In each, one could understand how upward progression is conspicuous and the condition of total effect once again returns to धनुः श्रेष्ठ. The significance of such a formation will have a necessary introspection into figural advancement and the formal method of arrangement. Once we obtain comprehensibility, we can also invent standard of value in each and every word, hence धनुः श्रेष्ठ, सज्यं, द्विजोत्तम and सत्यमुक्तं

each contains similar function for the sake of an upgradation of the universal and divine.

Inquisition constructed through the figural authority and the enactment of concrete universal could be substantially the occasions in which the structuralist paradigm could be fixed up as the primary necessity of functionality of the artistic situation. The evolution of signifiers completes the process of addition of required value. Thus when two lexicons move towards each other in the background of an appropriate communicative urgency, one could find truth and reality in the artistry. In the following verses, from Ādiparva of the *Mahābhārata* similarity of contention is obtained as a rule:

तद् अर्जुनो वीर्यवतां सदर्पस,
तद ऐन्दिर्रिइन्द्रावरज-प्रभावः।
सज्यं च चक्रे निमिषान्तरेण,
शरांश च जग्राह, दशार्ध-संख्यान्॥

विव्याध लक्ष्यं निपपात तच्च,
छिद्रेण भूमौ सहसाति-बिद्धम्।
ततोऽन्तरिक्षे च बभूव नादः,
समाज-मध्ये च महान् नि-नादः ॥ – 2.26, 27

tada arjuno vīryavatāṁ sadarpasa,
tada endirriindrāvaraja-prabhāvaḥ ।
sajyaṁ ca cakre nimiṣāntareṇa,
śarāṁśa ca jagrāha, daśārdha-saṁkhyān ॥

vivyādha lakṣyaṁ nipapāta tacca,
chidreṇa bhūmau sahasāti-biddham ।
tato 'ntarikṣe ca babhūva nādaḥ,
samāja-madhye ca mahān ni-nādaḥ ॥

Here movement of Arjuna towards the desired location for the sake of accomplishment of the task is worthy of attention. By his extraordinary mastery, he embodies in him a blessing. Thus he is in a position to hold the bow, hence mounts an arrow on the bow. The description for the purpose has synchronic assertion and therefore the fact of communication is generated in both the addresser and the addressee. For example, he explicates the medium by conferring concrete signifiers hence come to terms with the bow (सज्यं च चक्रे निमिषान्तरेण). With this addition of content the movement of signifiers becomes extraordinary and ultimately we must see how universal is asserted through "शरांश च जग्राह, दशार्ध-संख्यान्". Even beyond this, metaphorical communication is obtained in विव्याध लक्ष्यं निपपात तच्च, छिद्रेण भूमौ सहसाति-बिद्धम्।. In this विव्याध is the principal factor that governs the resolution and consequence of conjunction; thus छिद्रेण भूमौ सहसाति-बिद्धम् is propositionally excellent. Both the units and parts proceed to the universal with the transformation of the each into the concrete and thus we have ततोऽन्तरिक्षे च बभूव नाद: and also समाज-मध्ये च महान् नि-नाद:. What, in fact, we could perceive is the rise of signification at the elementary level and with the assorted contemplation, it moves over to the secondary situation and from there constructs the worth to enrich the whole artistry, hence could be presumed to be transmitting itself. For these reasons, the structuralist system will carry profoundity of assertion in the *Mahābhārata* and really it truthfully illustrates the interrelations between the universal experience and equally the universal language.

The synthesis of formative structures has diverse applications and there is also a systematic and regular exposition of content and medium. In fact, it is better to say that comprehension of the universal situation forms a variety of meaning-oriented conduct for the inscribed signifiers. In the *Rāmāyaṇa*, the idea of formalisation of value by first disintegrating the value and at a later stage calling forth the appropriate contents to reassert exact value, is brought to presentation. The gods and goddesses and other divine characters transform themselves into their earthly equivalents and perform every conceivable action to come to terms with every material situations of the world. Yet the accomplishment is so precise and perfect that one is really amazed at the brilliance of the presentation. The methodology of structuralist application on the text would absolutely be in the manner of what could be the best instance of understanding the comprehensibility of the entire situation. For example, look at Bālakāṇḍa of the *Rāmāyaṇa*:

> कोसलो नाम मुदितः स्फीतो जनपदो महान्।
> निविष्टः सरयूतीरे प्रभूतधनधान्यवान्।।
>
> तां तु राजा दशरथो महाराष्ट्रविबर्धनः।
> पुरीमावासयामास दिवि देवपतिर्यथा।। – 1.5, 9
>
> *kosalo nāma muditaḥ sphīto janapado mahān* ।
> *niviṣṭaḥ sarayūtīre prabhūtadhanadhānyavān* ।।
>
> *tāṁ tu rājā daśaratho mahārāṣṭravibardhanaḥ* ।
> *purīmāvāsayāmāsa divi devapatiryathā* ।।

This situation upholds the validity of an artistry that sustains continuous movements towards the objects and also away from the object so much so that the displacements and replacements both have a necessary projection in meaning. The applicability of positional signifiers at the every beginning is excellent and accordingly syntactical forms appear in their noteworthy intention, hence we have कोसलो नाम मुदितः स्फीतो जनपदो महान्. This presentation survives and acquires a configuration that is primarily explicated on the grounds of proportional cognition. The aspects of condition and terms approve themselves with the consistency of change, therefore the subject at the beginning conceives the object at the end. Hence कोसलो नाम being the subject presupposes an advertent rise in diachronic synthesis in the object, therefore, we have जनपदो महान् and also सरयूतीरे प्रभूतधनधान्यवान्. What, in fact, is happening is that the production of the contents gethers up synthesised space and margin in every word that appears as a correspondence of cumulation of the facts. It could be seen as the aspect of primary strength that has been built to actual synthesis. It is also a situation that contemplates the creation of actually realised centre or functional meaning in each of the syntactical forms developed in the foregoing observation. The verses of the *Rāmāyaṇa* are important not only for the sake of their rich content implication but also for the speed of transformation intended therein.

The passage of Śrī Rāma into the exile has brought about great calamities and sufferings for the whole of Bhāratavarṣa and accordingly, Bharata, who considers himself to be primarily responsible for the terms of the exile (his mother Kaikeyī wanted him to become the crown prince of Ayodhyā, hence the queen therefore, forced Daśaratha to yield to the promise he had made to her once upon a time) laments inconsolably. The lamentation of Bharata in having thus confirmed the perfection of the filial bond. The following verses from Ayodhayākāṇḍa of the *Rāmāyaṇa* may be considered:

उवाच भरतश्चित्रं धार्मिको धार्मिकं वचः।
कोहि स्यादीद्रशो लोको याद्रशस्त्वमरिंदम।।

न त्वां प्रव्यथयेद् दुःखं प्रीतिर्वा न प्रहर्षयेत्।
संमतश्चापि वृद्धानां तांश्च पृच्छसि संशयान्।। – 3.2, 3

uvāca bharataścitraṁ dhārmiko dhārmikaṁ vacaḥ ।
kohi syādīdraśo loko yādraśastvamarindam ।।

na tvāṁ pravyathayed duḥkhaṁ prītirvā na praharṣayet ।
saṁmataścāpi vr̥ddhānāṁ tāṁśca pr̥cchasi saṁśayān ।।

In this the paradigmatic application of the signifiers converts the relational forms into functional contents. Thus a synthesis is prepared for the sake of revival. Two things are definitely remarkable and would bear consistency of formulation and projection. In the first place, Bharata confirms the idea that centrality of signification has to be instructed to the principal function, and accordingly, shift in the relationship of signifiers is actually the essence of the strength of the content rather than making him appear. He foregrounds himself and makes the universality of Śrī Rāma to mark its appearance. The movements of sign justify the lengthening of lamentation, yet the effects are precise and locative. The acts of shifting, expunging and combining do not unsettle the proposition as such. On the whole, point would stand that the signification of Rāma as being universal and absolute is permanently styled through the process of dispersion and reversion, while it disperses, its intends transformation through proportionate variants. Similarly, while it reverts, it synthesises the wholesome attributes accordingly, न त्वां प्रव्यथयेद् दुःखं प्रीतिर्वा न प्रहर्षयेत becomes a significant addition to the total prospects of meaning that is evolving and is due to come up. What in fact, is happening, is that the expansion of opening resolution in which Bharata puts forth a truth regarding the greatness of Śrī Rāma and realises the truth in a concrete universal. Afterwards, the associative intention on the part of the word is so immensely powerful that the entire figural metaphor is directly stated and accordingly in the end we get समंतश्चापि वृद्धानां तांश्च पृच्छसि संशयान्. The accommodation of structure totally confers a value upon the functions and thus imitates a logical speculation about the whole.

Composition of functional sign in structuralist poetics remains one of the major advancements in the area of meaning intention. The progress of an artistry on account of enrichment and expansion in figurative as well as formal details like metaphor, metonomy, simile and the like creates the universal situation. In the *Mahābhārata* and the *Rāmāyaṇa*, the richness and strength of wholesome forms suggest that these would be a typical conjugation between the idealised words therefore every word is typically ideational, hence obtains a condition of universality. In the *Mahābhārata*, especially the functional attributes of the linguistic system and the methodological constructs of the artistic whole have an equal displacement towards transformation and accordingly there is a revival of the absolute in them. On the other hand, in the *Rāmāyaṇa* the artistry has a typical motif of conjunction. Hence the proportion of idealisation substantially approves the manner and quality of enrichment. It might be a fact to be mentioned that the property of sign is simultaneously emotive and intellectional, therefore, the index of manifestation that comes up after modification of an object expresses the largest context of the meaning. It must be brought within the range of extension, conformity and observation that morphologically and artistically the actual conditions really go a long way in purporting intensity in the generation of qualitative contents. For example, in the following verses from Kiṣkindhākāṇḍa of the *Rāmāyaṇa*, the expression of the content receives fair amount of intensity:

> अयं स कालः संप्राप्तः समयोऽध जलागमः।
> संपश्य त्वं नभो मेघैः संवृतं गिरिसंनिभैः।। – 5.2
>
> *ayaṁ sa kālaḥ saṁprāptaḥ samayo 'dha jalāgamaḥ* ।
> *saṁpaśya tvaṁ nabho medhaiḥ saṁvr̥taṁ girisaṁnibhaiḥ* ।।

In these verses Śrī Rāmacandra is configuring an intention to obtain a suggestive realisation of experience, hence he is longing to meets Sītā. The context corresponds to a valid measure in transformation, accordingly the object and the subject; addresser and addressee; speaker and listener; medium and content dispose themselves to the richness and strength of total artistic situation. In putting forth an utterance, "अयं स कालः संप्राप्तः समयोऽध जलागमः". Śrī Rāmacandra confirms an application in which words have a direct visibility and because of that a sequence is established from which an experience akin to longing is successfully established. The purport of romanticism is stratified accordingly in the non-hearers and the speaker, the essence is preferentially created through a direct address. It is, moreover, the term of association through paradigmatic function that the address is expressed in the form of truth and reality. The signification of rain as being the harbinger of goodness, well-being, union so on and so forth, is typically content in the adequate correlations that are there. Like, for example, mountain and the sky descending down the mountain. In this the growth of content through evolution or in other words the assimilation of synchrony could be understood. The sky and the mountain finally get transformed into the rain suggesting the universalisation of experience in causing the union of object with subject or subject with object. It must be remarkable to understand as to how the growing structures explicate evidence in favour of the requiring term of projection, for example, अयं स काल: is a native function that could be described to be vocative intersection of concrete syntax. On that account, when it is realised, it contracts a deep structural association with an extended metaphor in समयोऽध जलागम: while, on the other hand, the similarity in hyper-active syntax leads to both consequence and effect of the meaning and, accordingly, in other vocative that brings forth regeneration by proliferating the means and apparatus of expansion. Thus, संपश्य is truly an illustration of the fact. The structuralist circumstances that we comprehend are basically assimilative in nature inasmuch as the growing structure (in terms of syntax, morphology, phonology and semiotics) intends compulsory elevation in the circumstances of function and the largest situation that we could propose for the sake of modification and changes come to have a compulsory evolution. It doesn't matter how and why changing the structure of word, letter, syllable, paragraph, sentence brought forth a new function for the sake of the generation of an exclusive value, or, for that matter, the meaning. There might be certain conditions in which the length of signifier becomes so enlarged that the resultant value structure could almost be either infinite or otherwise, be beyond temporal causation. Consider the following from Yuddhakāṇḍa of the *Rāmāyaṇa*:

सर्वदा सर्वभूतानां नास्ति मृत्युरलक्षण:।
तव तद्वदयं मृत्युर्मैथिलीकृत लक्षण:।। – 6.29

sarvadā sarvabhūtānāṁ nāsti mṛtyuralakṣaṇaḥ।
tava tadvadayaṁ mṛturmaithilīkṛta lakṣaṇaḥ।।

The effect of causation concludes an affirmative reason for perception and, on that account, causation of empirical forms is quiet obvious. सर्वदा सर्वभूतानां proposes an extension of evolution, and, therefore, मैथिली is a synthesis of necessary cognitive forms. This would mean that intensification in the parol activity will have optimum generation of paradigmatic constituents in नास्ति मृत्युरलक्षण: मृत्युर्मैथिलीकृत लक्षण:. The choice and the suitability of the intention invents an absolutely heterogeneous conjunction in मैथिली, hence मैथिली, in itself, as a supreme metaphorical activity leading to the brilliance of observation. From other standpoint as well, the verses appear to be excellently disposed to bring about the purity of structural function. For example, we can understand how continuity of generative correspondence is maintained with revival and generation. Accordingly सर्वदा सर्वभूतानां नास्ति मृत्युरलक्षण: has associative excellence inasmuch as the string of concatenation we receive in सर्वदा सर्वभूताना and नास्ति मृत्युरलक्षण:. सर्वदा सर्वभूतानां expand the lexis towards timeless synthesis while नास्ति मृत्युरलक्षण: resolves the proposition through antithesis of inconsequential time and rewards. Addresser, addressee relationship is also to be recognised as evidence to support the value formation through the commuted function of the structures. Mandatory acting at the behest of an addresser transforms the paradigmatic constituents around Rāvaṇa the addressee and similarly नास्ति मृत्युरलक्षण: and मृत्युर्मैथिलीकृत लक्षण: become precisely the absolute injunction through which one has to understand the transformation or creation of meaning and that is quiet rightly the annihilation of Rāvaṇa and his clan. Structuralist motif puts forth assimilative point of view with regard to comprehensibility and construction of artistic models and category. The completion of functional assignment to the categories remains one of the objects through which the enrichment of categories could be brought to the level of intersection. Thus, the categories that participate, are precisely introduced into this environment. Sign, for example, is an act of revival of potential values and similarly when motif of a particular sign is generated there is a large-scale mutation in the morphological structure of the situation and from this phonology and syntax are similarly accentuated. Such a property is relevant to the controlled organisation of entire formation because in each the priorities of analytical circumstances, synthetical events are assured. In the *Rāmāyaṇa*, this part of structuralist poetics is immediately brought to recognition when the cyclical progression of an idea is logically elevated to the status of a pure fact. Śrī Rāma himself purifies the order of presentation of universal values and this, as a sign, is quite imminent to conform to the motif of truth and fact. Look at, for example, Yuddhakāṇḍa of the *Rāmāyaṇa*:

या मयासीन्न संबुद्धा कदाचिदपि मंदया।
पिता दानवराजो मे भर्ता मे राक्षसेश्वर:।।
पुत्रो मे शक्रनिर्जेता इत्यहं गर्विता भृशम्। – 6.39

yā mayāsīnna saṁbuddhā kadācidapi mandayā ।
pitā dānavarājo me bhartā me rākṣaseśvaraḥ ।।
putro me śakranirjetā ityahaṁ garvitā bhṛśaṁ ।

Here the process of conversion of refined object into refined subject is an event of deduction, and therefore, it strengthens the need of universal framework to affect the resolution. Mandodarī having had recognition of the fact that evil had been defeated and the truth had triumphed admits the mutability of consumptive signifiers and accordingly considers the evolution of signifiers through inductive means. Thus, her father (the king of demons), her husband (the god of demons), and her son (the universal warrior) have become separable by deformation into plunder and ruin. In this way, the constitutive proportion of the sign does much help in reviving either of these. On the other hand, deformative strength evolves the logical synthesis all along. In this way, the diachronic injunctions inherent in the deformative sign, project themselves along the process of evolution and the meaning is at once obtained that truth is the reality of analysis while evil is only synthetical in nature. In these conditions, the possibility is sustained and also realised for the sake of approval of commitment. In the work of art operative conditions which bring about purity and refinement are also necessarily those which initiate a long yet confirmed procedure of organisation and synthesis. For the similar reasons, function of sign upgrades the strength of artistry by shifting and combining the extraordinary value events.

The consequence of evolution in terms of presentation of different structures of a work of art creates an important facet of the functionality, therefore, within the framework established for such a purpose, the possibility of having refined additive or multiplicative figures is always existing. For example, look at Ayodhyākāṇḍa of the *Rāmāyaṇa*:

क्व चारण्यं क्व च क्षात्रं क्व जटाः क्व च पालनम्।
ईदृशं व्याहतं कर्म न भवान्कर्तुमर्हसि।। – 3.18

kva cāraṇyaṁ kva ca kṣātraṁ kva jaṭāḥ kva ca pālanam।
īdṛśaṁ vyāhataṁ karma na bhavānkartumarhasi।।

In this, Bharata questions the wisdom of Śrī Rāma in going into the exile and, accordingly, the content of inquisition supplements the model for growth that is otherwise underlying the whole discourse. The commencement of inquisition through appropriate terms of address invests a substance of expansion, and, thus, addresser and addressee correspond to coordinated mutation. On the other hand, the signifiers present themselves for the sake of both, addition and multiplication, and thus the beginning — क्व चारण्यं क्व च क्षात्रं क्व जटाः क्व च पालनम्. It would mean that the progression of extraordinary morphological propriety is not only cyclical but reversible as well, and the position of each inquisition seems to be at the centre of the entire cyclical formations. क्व चारण्यं is a fact presented for the sake of revival and acquisition of purity and therefore could appropriately hold on to the requirement of the meaning that is precisely ईदृशं व्याहतं कर्म न भवानकर्तुमर्हसि. While we examine the presented content it must appear to ourselves that thinking obtains all the necessary correlatives via consistency in the growth of inquisitive form inasmuch as, with each, the intensity is squarely mounted. Thus, diachronic variants go on bringing about consolidated addition to their structure. The entire scheme could be successfully presented along the following Saussurian graphics:

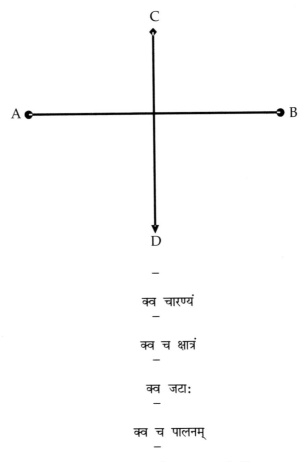

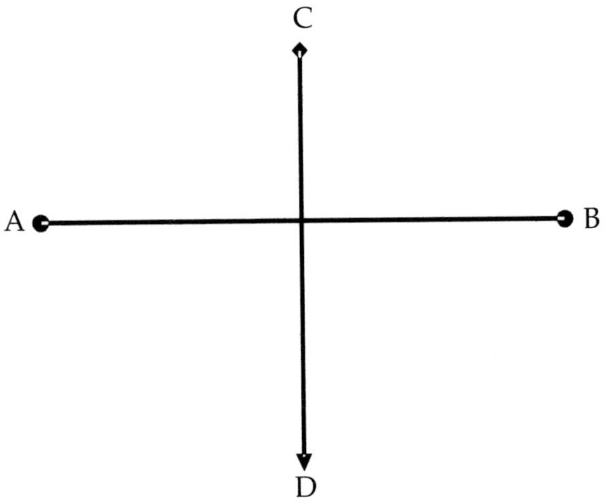

–

क्व चारण्यं

–

क्व च क्षात्रं

–

क्व जटा:

–

क्व च पालनम्

–

ईदृशं व्याहतं कर्म न भवानकर्तुमर्हसि

The content of evolution proposes structure for total value, thus we can understand how the act of inquisition gathers up and transmutes elementary morphological forms into total semiotic universal, and, on that account, one inquisition, in fact, modifies all the artistic materials available in that particular situation. In both the *Mahābhārata* and the *Rāmāyaṇa* the significance of actual content is so rich that extent of performance is equal to the intensity of composition. Hence structuralist effect is the reality of any consequence that one should like to have for the purpose of analysis.

The execution of structuralist ideals seems to be of considerable importance in those artistic formations where substitution of the categories is excellent. In Bhāsa's Sanskrit dramas (a dramatist of Indian tradition belonging to the period third century BCE), the characteristics of artistry are very well executed. The characterisation and plot construction, both appear to be done with an emphasis on an advancement of substitution or displacement. Yet, in either of the cases, the generation of high artistry is at once imminent. In *Svapnavāsavadattam*, for example, the presentation of the semantic ideals presupposes the synthesis of object into subject and subject into object and accordingly an excellent groundwork emerges for the comprehension of structuralist situation; for example, look at *Svapnavāsavadattam* of Bhāsa:

कस्यार्थः कलशेन मे मृगयते वासो यथानिश्चिंत
दीक्षां पारितवान किमिच्छति पुनर्देयं गुरोर्यइ भवेत।
आत्मानुग्रहमिच्छतीह नृषजा धर्माभिरामप्रिया
यद् यस्यास्ति समात्सितं वदतु तत् कस्याद्य किं दीयताम्।। – 1.8

kasyārthaḥ kalaśena me mṛgayate vāso yathāniścinta
dīkṣāṁ pāritavāna kimicchati punardeyaṁ guroryai bhavet ।
ātmānugrahamicchatīha nṛṣajā dharmābhi rāmapriyā
yad yasyāsti samātsitaṁ vadatu tat kasyādya kiṁ dīyatām ।।

In this episode, it is at once clear that the preparations are going on to get Udayana married once again to the princess of Magadha so that he could be brought back to the order of performance of the kingly ideals from which he seems to have deviated. The environment that has been presented confirms the excellence of wonder and curiosity by forcing every conviction to the conclusion, and, for that matter, the inquisitions are also at the same time the projection of paradigmatic and syntagmatic construction of the events. When

Kauñcakīya says कस्यार्थः कलशेन को मृगयते वासो यथानिश्चितं the realisation becomes immediate that the conversion of surprise into wonder and wonder into curiosity is at the back of the temporary invention that Kauñcakīya has undertaken. It is in this regard that effect revolves and rotates and ultimately once again originates with a promise to fulfil every gap and that also completes the evolution of the semantic terms inasmuch as inquisition is received at the logical end of the situation. "यद् यस्यास्ति समात्सितं वदतु तत् कस्याद्य किं दीयताम्" the passage also presents the range and variety of brilliant creative formulation, hence कस्यार्थः किमिच्छति and कस्याद्य are substantially the parole investing the whole of morphological apparatus and reviving the larger universal in which the actual significance of romance is contained. Even otherwise, the qualitative function of love directs ethical and moral enrichment, hence, the evolution of primary experience into secondary experience as a rule inheres in the whole function of artistry. We can understand that the performance and projection as being exceptionally significant in the following verses from *Svapnavāsavadattam* of Bhāsa:

पूर्व व्वयाप्यभिमतं गतमेवमासी
च्छलाध्यं गमिष्यसि पुनर्विजयेन भर्तुः।
कालक्रमेण् जगतः परिवर्तमाना
चक्रारपङ्क्तिरिव गच्छति भाग्यपङ्क्तिः।। – 1.4

pūrva vvayāpyabhimataṁ gatamevamāsī
cchalādhyaṁ gamiṣyasi punarvijayena bharthuḥ ।
kālakrameṇ jagataḥ parivartamānā
cakrārapaṅktiriva gacchati bhāgyapaṅkti ।।

Here the structural form elevates the degree of dissociation between cohesive content and therefore every morphological unit invents greater synthesis. Accordingly, when Yaugandharāyana says पूर्व व्वयाप्यभिमतं गतमेवमासी he should like to put forth an empirical view of the matter by constituting a direct modification of object into subject. Similarly, Vāsavadattā who has been lonely in being not in a position to meet Udayana feels being lonely. In these circumstances, the worth of association intends a thorough going change in the total system and we can notice that the movement of the words begins as an effect to enhance the displacement of time, of course, in a clockwise direction. For this purpose the employment of a metaphor in चक्रारपङ्क्तिरिव appears to be exceptionally brilliant. This derives from the idea that metaphorical injunction continues the activity of synthesis, hence Yaugandharāyana offers series of hopes and promises for the sake of better future of Vāsavadattā. The verses in the middle in which promise and hope are stated, gives a cyclical formulation to the entire thought structure and moreover the effect of modification of content into context is also exceptional — च्छलाध्यं गमिष्यसि पुनर्विजयेन भर्तुः। What, in fact, is happening is that the achievement of Bhāsa seems to be his ability to present a focus on reality rather than deviating from the reality. This reality is governed through multiple morphological and semantic divisions. For example, at the beginning one can understand the exact determination in what Yaugandharāyana speaks of गतमेवमासी and immediately qualifies this reality by interpretating situational variants in the form of च्छलाध्यं and कालक्रमेण्. The movement of qualitative variants confirms a necessary formation of the whole. The structuralist condition is understood to be finding its worth in the continuity of enrichment and refinement proposed and suggested by the semantic and syntactical function of the lexicons. While we move further in the drama, the advancement of structure is really unusual and concrete. For example, look at the *Svapnavāsavadattam* of Bhāsa:

विस्त्रब्धं हरिणाश्चरन्त्यचकिता देशागतप्रत्यया
वृक्षाः पुष्फलैः समृद्धविटपाः सर्वे दयारक्षितः।

भूयिष्ठं कपिलानि गोकुलधनान्य क्षेत्रवत्यो दिशो

निःसन्दिग्धमिदं तपोवनमयं धूमो हि बह्वाश्रयः॥

vistrabdhaṁ hariṇāścarantyacakitā deśāgatapratyayā
vṛkṣāḥ puṣphalaiḥ samṛddhaviṭapāḥ sarve dayārakṣitaḥ ।

bhūyiṣṭhaṁ kapilāni gokuladhanānya kṣetravatyo diśo
niḥsandigdhamidaṁ tapovanamayaṁ dhūmo hi bahvāśrayaḥ ॥

In this event, the perfection of an indivisible situation in which we can observe completeness of meaning, comes to our comprehension. The beginning is remarkable and ब्रह्मचारी (*brahamacārī*) understands the constitutive excellence proposed and offered by the location. The reality offered by the content and the meaning suggested by the evolution of content into context explicates the essential virtue underlying the whole thing. In being able to understand, "विस्त्रब्धं हरिणाच्श्ररन्त्यचकिता देशागतप्रत्यया, the speaker presents the balance and poise of universal configuration of the morphology. विस्त्रब्धां is a consequence of bliss invariably inducted into the situation by concomitance. Similarly, हरिणाच्श्ररन्त्यचकिता is a conviction that attends to the modification of object into subject and subject into object. The dramatist situates the largest comprehensible variety of meaning by insisting the wholesome form into each of the contents. Accordingly, the observation सर्वे दयारक्षितः could manifest both recognition and reversal in that it manifests the resolution in निःसन्दिग्धमिदं तपोवनयं, the semiotic function has also an equally direct visibility and for this purpose deer, trees, cows, and fruits and the smoke emitted by the pyre adopt a significance to upgrade the worthiness of the situation. We can also offer to conceive a growth of the context and content along the triangular scheme of presentation and for that matter the aboard of learning is at the centre while the other entities are in direct proportion to the situation. This would be quite comprehensive with regard to the view that the morphological forms constitutive at the centre are the enriched derivatives of the peripheral units having a concentrative occurrence; thus the instance of synchrony and diachrony would be immediately imminent and the structuralist situation would also be at once imminent.

Structuralist poetics is primarily a procedural enrichment of the morphological, phonological, semantic, semiotic and syntactic units which, out of necessity, come to occupy a place of conspicuous presence in the artistic formation. In each of these forms, the division of qualitative situation is in the manner of primary and secondary injunction, and, therefore, a good deal of possibility is observed in so far as modification potentials are concerned. A category in its primary form has to be modified and what will modify must be the qualitative excellence inherent in each in an open ended figuration. Consequently there would be considerable activity purporting division, addition, subtraction and multiplication and simultaneously there would also be the beginning of evolution as a necessary event to complete the process of creation of the absolute. While we made an application of the structuralist poetics on canonical forms, we primarily went by the structural consideration and results and the conclusions were extraordinarily brilliant and remarkable. Great Indian texts offer equally greater perception of the categories involved in the conjunction of the human existence. Thus, there had been the possibility of bringing about an appreciation of such texts in terms of concretisation they undergo by an empirical series of changes. Towards the end, one really understands the worth and imminence of the universality.

II

Dhvani system of Indian poetics deals with the nature, forms, functions and the objects of artistic categories involved in the creation of an ideal artistic environment. To this end, it also creates methodical procedure to conceive and enrich such categories as *śabda, pada, varṇa, vākya, bhāva, vibhāva, anubhāva, sthāyībhāva, sañcārībhāva,* etc. There are two distinct orders in which the entire procedure is accomplished. In the first place, selection of those categories, which are capable of being transformed, is made and in the second place, concentrated and thoroughly organised device of enrichment is introduced into the situation, and accordingly, towards the end we have concrete universal in respect of each of these. It would mean, therefore, that the meaning emerges as the fundamental instrument through which universality is obtained and to achieve this end multiple divisions are made in the artistic formation and each of such divisions accords a specific apparatus and environment to the meaning. In the primary stages, the meaning is only significant but with development of artistry it acquires a distinction of being absolute. It could be seen that activity leading to the constitution of absolute is also one that proposes metaphor, metanomy and other figural devices as being legitimate vehicles of the situation of transformational activity. In fact, *śabda* and *artha* encompassing letters, syllables and the sentence on the one hand and thought, language, experience on the other, are brought to the terms of synthesis and modification and consequently there is the universal in respect of each. It is also worth noticing that the devices of enrichment and absolute anticipate progressive correlation and multiple coalescements, and, on that account, there is definitely the fact of evolution that comes to be associated with the whole situation. We can understand that absolute universal, refinement, and concretisation are the end products of an artisic situation that is thus obtained. In the following passages we would like to illustrate the significance of this fact by taking into consideration the great Western poetic texts as being the worthy objects of application of the profundity of *dhvani* theory.

Homer's *Iliad* happens to be at the centre of poetical activity that was to be undertaken in the later years in the Western world. The greatness of *Iliad* lies not only in the fact that it is the first European epic but also in the manner in which it expounds a structure for mortal and immortal existence. While

Homer speaks of a war between the Greek and the Trojan for the sake of Helen in which nearly all the gods of antiquity were worthy participants. Besides, on an equal scale, there was a magnificent participation by the great warriors who enjoyed a direct and first-hand communication and correspondence with the gods. Homer chooses the circumstances to speak of man as man and man as god, god as god and god as man and finally war as destruction, revival and regeneration as well. In the first book of *Iliad,* Homer speaks of the following situation:

> Achilles' baneful wrath — reasoned, O goddess that empos'd
> Infinite sorrows on the Greeks, and many brave souls loosd
> From breasts heroic; sent them for, to that invisible cave
> That no light comforts; and their limbs to dogs and vultures gave:
> To all which Jove's will gave effect; from whom first strife begun
> Betwixt Atrides, King of men, and Thetis god like son.
>
> — I. 1-10

Here, we can understand how the artistry is proposed and grows in such a way that every morphological condition and situation involves consummation. The immediate reverses in the war are perfectly built around the opposition between Achilles and Agamemnon and what comes in consequences is nearly a complete artistry. The phrases "baneful wrath", and "infinite sorrows" finally perform the act of mutation and these combine and divide, multiply and substract and etablish the idea for the sake of universal effect. What in fact is happening is that the richness and texture of "baneful wrath" and "infinite sorrows" is so much so that the whole formation finally merges into the complete whole and the conditionalities of *dhvani* are immediately obtained. It is, in fact, *vivakṣitavācya* sort of *dhvani*. In Homer, the proportion of enriched content and the necessity of displaying the configuration of a strengthened artistry, both go hand in hand. The war between the Greeks and the Troy and hence the figures who participate, including the female ones, themselves become the models through which the natural form of discourse is elevated and substantiated through an actually purified texture. In the above example "infinite sorrows" illustrates not only the purity of texture but how the compound syntax could be made to work as an approval of the highest observable artistic form. It in fact, recovers and disseminates varities of reason to finally synthesise and modify the whole situation. *Dhvani* is quite convincingly a way to purify the artistic form and substantiate the idea that the categories involved opt for transformation into their universal forms when and only when truth and reality of the content, context and the medium are proportionate to the intensity of reasonableness of the external objects. To this extent Homer's *Iliad* is the best example of the situation, look at the following:

> And now in the midst of the gathering of the Danaans then utterest thy prophecies, and declarest that forsooth it is for this cause that the god that smiteth afar is bringing woes upon them, for that I would not accept the glorious ransom for the maid, that daughter of Chryses, seeing I am minded for rather to keep her in my home. For, know you I prefer her before Clytemnestra, my wedded wife, since she is no whit inferior to her, either in form or in stature, or in mind, or anywise in handiwork. —I.110-15

In this passage the locative and non-locative conjunctions in the form of "and" and "that", "then", thy, "I" and the like create a foundation for the expansion of syntactical structures. Because of these the essential configuration of content is enlarged and the content is accordingly situated in the firmly strengthened morphological universal. Therefore "and", "then" and "you" immediately obtain the highest intensity in the modification and become enlarged for the sake of value and meaning that could be attached to them. In this way, we can understand that Agamemnon's fury over the possibility of losing Chryses is now turned into a method of inquisition that has a bearing on the prospect of war. Homer's ability in presenting ephemeral human emotion in the form of a concrete formation having the power of truth and reality creates, in fact, *vivakṣitavācya dhvani*. The way in which the modification is initiated from the primary insignificance to the secondary universality is also expressive of the fact that exceptional syntactical structure would invent a form of excellence for itself. In Homer, the application of *dhvani* will have two important characteristics. In the first place, it would let us know how the content proposed for syntax would ultimately be the carriers of massive artistic significance. While, on the other hand, it will have the capability of initiating a division so that evolution of the units could be successfully undertaken. For example, look at Homer's *Iliad*:

> So saying, he sprang upon him, and seized him by the helmet with thick crest of horse — hair, and whirling him about began to drag him towards the well — greaved Achaens; and Paris was choked by the richly — broidered strap beneath his soft throat, that was drawn tight beneath his chin to hold his helm. — III. 370-75

Here actual style of inventing the words and the realistic manner of concatenating them along a smooth and vertical graph explains the maturity of intellection. What, in fact, happens is that the nominal and pronominal syntactical situations are superimposed and the addition is invented through a passive formation, accordingly, the time of action, place of action and content of action each become so well synthesised that absolute suggesting *vivakṣitavācya* is at once imminent. One of the things that is to be noticed while reading Homer's *Iliad* is that there is a greater concentration of conjunction and that precisely adds to the simplicity of the style. While, on the other hand, every conjunction is capable of bringing about varieties of synthesis and transformation, and in every transformation one can understand how appropriateness of lexicon is equal to the absolute that is ensuing. The growth of lexicon is primarily a fact suggested in the graduation for the sake of identification of the strengthened circumstances of evolution. Once the identification is made, the characterisation conducive to the emergence of universal is strongly manifested. We cannot afford to deny the fact that actual arrangement of the participating content is intended to obtain figural modifications at once and immediately if the context has brought forth the suitability of enrichment. In Homer, the ideational events lie conspicuous than the magnificence of figural modification and that too with the support enlisted through the designated and noteworthy conjunction. This function of Homeric artistry is really very promising for the sake of theoretical plan generated in *dhvani* formulation. *Dhvani* holds a canon for the formal and figural universality by revising the content of every category that comes to participate in the artistic formation. For example, consider *Iliad*:

> And Hector grasped and bore a stone that lay before the gate, thick at the base, but sharp at the point; not easily might two men, the mightiest of the folk, have upheaved it from the ground upon a wain — men, such as mortals now are — yet lightly did he wield it even alone; and the son of crooked — counselling Cronos made it light for him. And as when a shepherd easily beareth the flee of a ram, taking it in one hand, and but little doth the weight thereof burden him; even so Hector lifted up the stone and bare it straight against the doors that guarded the close and strongly fitted gates — double gated they were, and high, and two cross bars held them within, and a single bolt fastened them.
>
> — XII.445-55

Homer intends a consequence through just and upright presentation of an action in which Hector is paving a way for his progress. The rationalisation of object purported for the description gives us an idea of sequence and chronology through which the transformation is intended. For example, "stone", "gate", and "ground" are the correlatives which provide an occasion for the change of an object into subject. The whole experience is so concentrated and so exact that the totality of effect is at once conceived. The beginning of the passage in, "And Hector grasped and bore a stone that lay before, the gate" one must understand how purity and precision of language brings forth the composite idea before us. The intention of the poet is to speak of the grace of Hector in traversing a path that had been so long nearly impossible for others and it is done with such a great success. The description of the stone in the next place is also well-worth noticing: "thick at the base but sharp at the point". Here an apportunity is provided to find out how the experience could be ratiocinated with the help of commonplace images, yet the purity could be not only hightened but universalised. Finally, because of sequence, chronology and effectiveness of the images *vivakṣitavācya* is at once evident.

The presentation of actual war accompanying a lot of deaths, bloodshed and beheadings amounting almost to ravages contained in the mutilation of the bodies has also its own brilliance:

> Now as long as it was morn and the sacred day was waxing, so long the missiles of either side struck home, and the folk kept falling; but at the hour when a woodman maketh ready his meal in the glades of a mountain, when his arms are grown tired with felling tall trees, and weariness cometh upon his soul, and desire of sweet food seizeth his heart, even then the Danaans by their valour brake the battalions, calling to their fellows through the lines. And among them

> Agamemnon rushed forth the first and slew a warrior, Bienor, shephered of the host, — himself and after him his comrade, Oileus, driver of horses. Oileus verily leapt down from his chariot and stood and faced him, but even as he rushed straight upon him the king smote him on the forehead with his sharp spear, nor was the spear stayed by his helm, heavy with bronze, but passed through it and through the bone, and all his brain was spattered about within; so stayed he him in his fury. These then did Agamemnon, king of men, leave there, gleaming with their naked breasts, when he had stripped off their tunics, and went on to slay Isus and Antiphus, two sons of Priam, one a bastard and one born in wedlock, the twain being in one car: the bastard held the reins, but glories Antiphus stood by his side to fight. These twain had Achilles on a time bound with fresh withes amid the spurs of Ida, taking them as they were herding their sheep, and had set them free for a ransom. But now the son of Atreus, wide ruling Agamemnon, struck Isus on the breast above the nipple with a cast of his spear, and Autiphus he smote hard by the ear with his sword, and cast him from the chariot. . . . And as a lion easily crusheth the little ones of a swift hind, when he hath seized them with his strong teeth, and hath come to their lair, and taketh from them their tender life, . . . even so was no one of the Trojans able to ward off destruction from there twain, but themselves were driven in flight before the Argives. — XI.85-120

Homer should like to contend that war is both cause and effect inasmuch as it destroys and revives. Accordingly, the warriors who put forth their valour and prowess seek to confirm their own attitude through the concentrated function of knowledge inherent in them as such. In this background, in the above passage, the war has started and great warriors have opened their arms against one another. Agamemnon being the greatest, rises and his rise is such that every great object of earth capable of manifesting itself is rising so that the deeds of bravery of Agamemnon could be enlisted upon the annals of chronicle eternally. This idea comes to us in the manner of a perfect sequence in which simile, metaphor and nearly every other figure of speech participates. The projection of truth is consistent obtaining full-scale description of the vigour of the warrier revealed in total destruction of the body of the enemy. For example, look at such description from the *Iliad*:

> Oileus verily leapt down from his chariot and stood and faced him, but even as he rushed straight upon him the king smote him on the forehead with his sharp spear, nor was the spear stayed by his helm, heavy with bronze, but passed through it and through the bone, and all his brain was spattered about within; so stayed he him in his fury. — XI.95-100

In this the consistency of expressed and felt realisation could be the events through which one proceeds to examine the necessity of bravery being chiefly illustrative in the optimum circumstances it carries in its ruthless fall upon the enemy. This condition is created for the harmonious progression of the circumstances for the sake of complete evolution leading ultimately to the meaning, thus *vivakṣitavācya* is conceived.

In Homer's *Iliad* the function of *dhvani* is, to identify, designate, classify and ultimately evolve the random category into a committed and truthful excellence from which the assurance of meaning is perfectly made.

The idea of extreme purity of the categories contained in the theory of *dhvani* finds an exceptionally good application in Dante's *Divine Comedy*. Ānandavardhana should like to mention that the primary function that must, of necessity, come up in an artistic formation is the rendering of participating categories into their purest equivalents in recognised expression. By "purity" Ānandavardhana has two important contentions to make. In the first place, it means the removal of primitive circumstances in which crudeness, essential and non-essential contents perform to invest the categories with inappropriate conjunction and conjugation. This, in turn, affects the process of refinement that is considered to be so essential in upgrading the categories to their universal form. Secondly, the enactment of truth and reality as being two complete additions to the growing formation, is also brought to the unnecessary inversion. This, therefore, has to be so constructed that the harmony of medium, content, context is maintained. In Dante's *Divine Comedy* the concept of good and bad comes to be stated or explained in terms of the divisions of intensity of goodness and badness in the manner of hell and heaven. According to Dante when an event is bad it is also something that corresponds to sin, and, in turn, sin is an affectation contained in the realisation of material temptation like wrath, greed, lust, like, dislike so on and so forth. For the communication of each there is an order of evil and every evil is ultimately resolved into damnation. The damnation is reversible and, therefore, one who is damned must suffer. The extent of suffering depends on the intensity of evil to which one had his/her bearing. Normally, it is spread over the space of infinity and the revocation is possible if one could infuse into oneself and convince the god of perpetual virtue in himself, yet, before this could come up, millions of years will have to pass. In Dante's ideology hell and heaven stand as two events of compatability, adoptability and transformability in that evil will have to be turned into virtue and virtue is rendered into an application of purer significance that will have finally bliss, hence communication with the god. The brilliance of such an attitudinal invention calls for a systematic analysis in terms of *dhvani*. Here are the opening lines of Dante's *Inferno*:

> In the middle of the journey of our life I [Came to] myself in a dark wood [Where] the straight way was lost, Ah! how hard a thing it is to tell what a wild, and rough, and stubborn wood this was, which in my thought renews the fear!
>
> — I.1-6

Dante considers the prospect of putting himself to the test of examination and evolution. For that matter, he subjects his soul to come out and adopt the procedural refinement through which he will have, at least, some peace. For this there is a graduation to compunction, examination and evaluation of sins and follies committed in the past. Consequently, the opening utterance is remarkable in which he says "In the middle of journey of our life I (myself) in a dark wood, the straight way was lost." In this he proposes to opt for truth as truth and reality as reality; he therefore compares and contrasts his individual existence, his private self and his subjective ethos against the absolute principles of purification and refinement. The individuality contained in him is primary while the absolute that is imminent is universal. Therefore, he will have to come to terms with realisation, comprehension, meditation and understanding so much so that he could understand that what is unworthy in him and could offer himself to canonisation. "I myself in a darkwood" is really expressive of brilliance of the poet in that it begins a commitment for realisation and also a submission to the higher form. On the other hand, the correlations, he employs in the form of ethical symbol, like "dark wood" and the like help him in purifying the whole situation. The beginning of the passage introduces the simplicity and clarity and even otherwise totality of conviction the poet has determined for the sake of himself and on account of himself, as also for having the understanding of peace that will bring forth knowledge. Such a progression in regard to individual existence would amount to having a reinvention of oneself in such a way that every individual dysfunction is carefully revealed and exposed for the sake of being considered fit for the whole thing. In other words, Dante's ability to understand himself as himself, locate himself within himself and finally discover himself to be as one who is really suffering configures the entire artistic model presented by him along the lines of assured evolution.

The idea of evolution is such that it changes the structural and functional forms underlying the individual. On every occasion, Dante speaks of having a direction towards "I". He also comprehends greater refinement by the virtue of a contrast that he brings forth by supplementing this "I" with "way". The injunction of "I" with "my" anticipates a consolidation in terms of the rearrangements of the contents. It could also be made to be the case in consideration that commonplace images and actual symbols effectively rotate themselves to the critical forms available in the life of an individual. For example "dark wood" symbolically intends inaccessibility and purports to suggest a darkness created by material affectation in which nearly everybody is lost. Such an achievement of the poet could contain a reliable argument for his greatness. What in fact happens is that Dante is really very successful in evolving the primary significance of the whole situation into universality and this case for *vivakṣitavācya* is truly substantiated.

Sometimes the purity of content is so universally ordered that inquisition and comprehension both become necessary consequences of observation. For example, look at the following verses from *Inferno*:

> The time was at the beginning of the morning; and sun was mounting up with those stars, which were with him when Divine love first moved those fair things: so that the hour of time and the sweet season [caused me to have good hope].
>
> — I. 37-41

Here Dante is finding out consolidated way to suggest how the effect of realisation and the resolution of realisation both have the strength of commonplace reality of the experience. Thus the observation begins with total confession in the natural delight of the things. The language employed for the purpose is consequential in terms of appropriate functionality that it achieves through images and symbols. For example, in the expression "*time was at the beginning of the morning*" Dante upholds the merit of feeling and thinking simultaneously so that there is the richness of heterogeneous inscription. The effect of language is such that it carries a medium in which the images grow to the extent of inclusion at every exact coordinate. The extent of simplicity is also remarkable inasmuch as every word is in itself a thoroughgoing experience of presentation. The further development of the same situation would bring forth the merit of examination:

> that animal with the gayskin; yet not so, but that I feared at the sight, which appeared to me, of a lion. A she-wolf, that looked full of all cravings her leanness; and has ere now made many live in sorrow. — I. 42-44, 49-51

Identification of an object as a mode of expression of an experience is, in fact, Dante's excellence. The material temptation intends a punishment from the god and thus the lion and the other animal, which are being spoken of by the poet, form a correlative for the sake of the prospective purgation. The sinner deserves punishment and the lion and the wolf are two agents, which are supposed to be punished. The realisation, acceptance and confession go hand in hand with the plain utterances made by the poet. The expressions of experience follow sequential arrangement and ultimately an organised whole emerges out of the concentrated process of refinement. The poet first chooses to speak of the subject (the fear of amazement and ultimately an organised whole emerges out of the concentrated fear of punishment) and the subject motivates the poet to introduce directly an assertive form. Secondly, the object-subject conjunction is made to be situated just after the completion of them and, lastly, the precision of experience comes forth as a result of addition of each into each. This could form a part of the idea that goes so excellently well in *dhvani*. Every unit of every category must enter into the relationship of harmony and correspondence in that every refined unit has to be refined. While this goes on, it leads to the creation of *dhvani* with an emphasis on significance and value. When Dante says, in the above passage, *"that animal with the gayskin, yet not so"*, he means to examine the exact structure of experience, and, therefore, towards the end he identifies the lion and the she-wolf to be too dreadful agents which are likely to punish the sinners. This would mean that the language finally evolves into an experience by opting and proposing concentrated variables for the sake of universalisation. This would, therefore, be an appropriate occasion to supplement *dhvani*.

Indexing of language and formation of wholesome experience could also be the situations through which we can understand how *dhvani* forms a case in point, for example, look at the following verses from the *Inferno*:

> When we met a troop of spirits, who were coming alongside the bank; and each looked coming at us, as in the evening men are wont to look at one another under a new moon; and towards us sharpened their vision, as an aged tailor does at the eye of his needle. — XV. 16-21

The idea of having the purgation is being considered as a prospect of moving into the better and the higher walks of life. For this purpose, Dante is considering the idea of having a comprehension of the various causes that might have led to damnation. To this end, the images, metaphor, symbol and the whole language constitute a sequence of evolution and finally the meaning is established as universal significance. Dante is now a damned spirit and the effect of damnation is compounded by the agony of other damned spirits. For this, the symbols are pure inasmuch as we have — *"aged tailor"*, *"sharpened their vision"*, *"eye of the needle"*. Each substantiates and synthesises the purity of the situation by inducing brightness, hardness, purity, elegance, reasonableness so on and so forth. The growth of an idea through the process of transmutation via absolute objects is something that we should like to assign to the idea of *vivakṣitavācya dhvani*.

The assimilation of concrete form and reasonable poetic circumstances also helps the poet in finding an appropriate medium for the expression of an experience. The significance of correspondence between emotive and linguistic categories (thought, language, experience, imagination, word, syllable, sentence, *bhāva*, *vibhāva*, *anubhāva*, *sañcārībhāva*, *sthāyībhāva*, *ālambana* and *uddīpana*) is so realistically manifested that the result produced in the end becomes an expression of purity embodied in truth, precision, elegance, brevity, rationality and the like. Consider the following verses from the *Inferno*:

> He began: "What chance, or destiny, brings thee, ere thy last day, down here? and who is this that shews the way?"
>
> "There above, up in the clear life, I lost myself", replied I, "in a valley, before my age was full". — XV. 46-50

In these passages, we can understand how the native situation could become an occasion of an expression of virtue in life and thus the experience explicates rationalised circumstances of inscription. Dante commands the truth by the virtue of being impeccably placed in exceptional condition of suffering. On the other hand, the spirit who is guiding him anticipates successful forebodings for him. Accordingly, the transformation is formulated. Curiosity becomes an intention and intention is naturalised into truth of being hopefully released from damnation. The manner of interposing object and subject is really significant in that it is brought about in the manner of commonplace conversation upholding the truth of the fact that even a damned soul, by a series of sufferings and punishments, could attain bliss in the forthcoming life. The implement of such situation is embodied in *"who is this that shews the way?"*, *"There above, up in the clear life, I lost myself"*, and finally *"in a valley, before my age was full"*. The combination of metaphorical material synthesises both the image and symbol and hence expresses the refined condition of experience. Such an analysis is, in fact, the imminence of *vivakṣitavācya dhvani*.

Dante's *Divine Comedy* illustrates the significance of *dhvani* in the manner in which it contains and embodies higher forms of modification of linguistic and emotive categories. Each such modification brings forth a refinement and each such refinement, in turn, is a way to universality of the situation.

Conclusion

FORMULATION of the theory of transformation in relation to the object and terms conceptualised in *dhvani* and the structuralist poetics invariably establishes a ground for the change of an object into event in which both are specific to the achievement of the highest intensity. In an artistic situation, the primary products are essentially generative in nature, therefore, the structure of the categories not only provides necessary strength but also conveys the whole form of the concerned category to reinvent a possibility for its inception as an order and system. In these two traditions, change, conversion, synthesis and evolution from an elementary form into a significant form is a phenomenon of organisation and obviously the cause of direction in which every content, every medium and every context has to be discreetly and distinctly located. This is realistically made with the emergence of linguistic and emotive foundations of the artistic situation, and, at that, the selection, combination and distribution of *śabda, pada, vākya, bhāva, vibhāva, sañcārībhāva, sthāyībhāva, anubhāva, ālambana* and *uddīpana* on the one hand and words, letters, syllables, sentences, paragraphs, thoughts, language, experience and imagination on the other hand are, of necessity, purported for the sake of assorting a consequence of exposition; thus interpretation comes to acquire proper values for themselves. The style of putting up appropriate configuration for the contents, is, in fact, a culmination of a series of long yet concise formation of the artistry. The situation intends, for the matter of that, when all the categories, contents and models have been gathered and stored up to meet a quality in significance. The evolution begins by suggesting systematic correlation and correspondence between the formative categories. Every enriched category is made to correspond and correlate to the similar situation on the other side of the situation. When correlatives and corresponding terms are readjusted against each other, the process of modification is finally complete. The view of matter adopted in such a condition is that the meaning is the beginning and end of the situations founded upon correlation, addition, multiplication and division. The issue of qualitative excellence is generally made to occupy the foremost position in changing the insignificance of primary order of imprecision. The ability to enact confirmed motives for such a persuit implicates the creation of universal standard. It is thus quite appropriate to say that the contention of evolution and intention to signify the order of value essentially brings about a vast range of meaning with attended network of medium and content-specific relations. The terms of unified projection supplementing the cause of concentrated aggregate is chiefly manifested through acquisition of perfection in the form and function of meaning, regeneration of text, efficiency of communication of the content, context and medium and comprehensibility of an assorted value of proto- and supra-imitative conjunctions. It is also remarkable that in each of these commitments to performance, the artistic situation reveals its merits in absolute conjunction.

II

Meaning is an event of transformation, and, therefore, one of the essential products of growth, organisation, development, expansion and enrichment of the participating contents and the categories of the artistic situation. In the creation of meaning preference is always accorded to the purpose of development and the manner of association. In *dhvani* and the structuralist poetics, meaning is recognised as an effect of precision in which the organisation and enrichment are not only maximum but attend to the achievement of cumulation and inversion. In *dhvani*, the function of linguistic and emotive models is mooted for the sake of the necessary inversion in such a way that *śabda, pada, vākya, bhāva, vibhāva* and *anubhāva* are strengthened and selected substantially to the newer positions in which the possibility to procure variants and equivalents or comprehension is essentially supreme. Once this process starts cumulating, the evidence of maturity of the contents becomes specific to an approval to universality of the concerned situation. It would immediately suggest that every category by now has obtained significance in terms of its own independence because of which there will be an addition of truth and reality to its existence. For that matter, every activity proceeds to convert itself into succession so much so that the sequence is established for the sake of an excessively rich perspective in terms of purposely succinct artistry. The underlying movement of the content is so thoroughly adequate that every instance of succession is further conceived in the intersection of emotive and linguistic model. Such an event of resolution invents maximum intensity of enrichment and organisation. There can be at least two concomitant divisions through which appropriateness that figures up in the wake of selection and distribution of the category could be successfully realised. In the first place, the convergence of the content into extraordinarily rich forms of context and synthesis of the categories into confirmed intents of progression bring about the functionality in the whole artistry. It must be understood that the ability of being functional relegates the inquisitive mode of variation, and, on that account, the rate of association and addition is enhanced to even an exceptionally high degree. With an arrangement like this the artistry becomes conspicuous and distinct by the presence of advertent poetic materials. The manner of evolution described in *dhvani* takes up the issues and problems of random distribution of the functional model of the artistry, and, therefore, Ānandavardhana goes on to suggest that the dispersal of the specified categories is only a beginning of the larger event of modification inasmuch as one principle or specific content carrying optimum resolution will be brought to act as the instrument of transformation. It does not matter, however diverse and deviant the application of the resolved model is, the competence and performance of the categories will be mutated appreciably through the circumstance of optimisation. In other words, the minor variables intending a change in the perspective will have to be multiplied in the presence of the principle function so as to yield a result conducive to the largeness of the artistry. For this reason *śabda*, *pada* and *vākya* or even *bhāva*, *vibhāva* and the like open themselves for the sake of random distribution, and while the event is going on the contents embodying the highest intensity are concretised in an altogether vigorous manner. Yet, each such action is accomplished through an agent that holds an exception of being the most significant. In the second place, revival of the position of junction confers an equal merit of enrichment on the different shades and aspects of linguistic and emotive models. The ideal artistry is thus rendered. In the structuralist system, the prospect of distribution of the categories is eminently fitted into the effect of modification. Here, words, letters and syllables on the one hand, experience, imagination and thought on the other, go on promoting a valid style of enrichment through addition and multiplication. The time that is supposed to be fixed upon the exposition and the recovery of the enriched models is also the time in which most of the signifiers are produced and created. In each of these signifiers, the inherence of an absolute form is justified inasmuch as every signifier constitutes an instrument for the equal concentration of phonological morphological, semantic and semiotic divisions. It would mean, in other words, that the event of signification is precisely the time in which the displacement towards authentic situation is complete while this displacement is manifested along the historical or other annals of time period; the area of expansion is considerably rich and high. For the matter of that, truth is factually evident in associating diachrony with the creation of the firmer modes of value and meaning sequence. Saussure, Barthes, Jakobson, Genette, Greimas have variously stated the condition of value performance to be necessarily equated with the association of the signifiers accruing as phonologically divergent and semantically congruent. In such a necessity of function, the end-result and end-products are bound to be stylistically cohesive with an authentic grasp on the medium and the context. The range and extent of clarifying the categories with regard to their projection into the scheme of enrichment depends on the fact that the sign derived from the particular context maintains a chronology for the sake of installing a signifier in the similar direction. The effect of presentation of the coherent signifiers is brought to maximum utilisation inasmuch as the range and extent of dispersion is implicit in the external/internal divisions of the artistry. To record the significant in such a way, a purpose has to be implanted by adding signifiers immediately and also by allowing the lapse of time in the process of addition. While the enactment of addition is a method of achieving the explicit result, leading to concept formation, the circumstances necessitated support the organisation of idealised contents with greater authority and renewed urgency. In both the systems, the presentative function and expository contention of the categories are constitutive of primary excellence and therefore, it would be possible to move the enriched categories towards interaction and transmogrification.

III

The composition of structure of meaning as an end-product of the evolution of the categories is an event of truth and thus accomplished successfully by such instruments of resolution as addition, division, multiplication, association, subtraction, conjunction, injunction, conception, inception and comprehension. In *dhvani*, the record of resolution surfaces extraordinarily in the substance of addition. The process of addition could be understood to be as the bringing together of two categories of diverse origin in which proximity would essentially lead to an enhancement of structure and function in the both. Ānandavardhana, Abhinavagupta, Mammaṭa and others have conclusively established the fact that when the categories are exposed for the sake of mutual identification they opt for internalisation of each into each. From this, the consideration of factual standard or higher variable incorporating an elevated scale of comprehension could be successfully understood. The urgency of throwing open the fact of artistic presentation could invariably launch a range of figurative and formal variations, and, for this reason, the procedure to add becomes very conspicuous. The description of *śabda* along point of time would initiate a long range of attendant contents with an equal enrichment, and similarly, the version of *bhāva* that is inscribed in the other side of division would approach approximately for the sake of successful evolution. This emphasis on concentrating the functional part in an equally functional part is further subjected to ratiocinated description. This would ultimately insist on a curriculum for the exact configuration of an artistry. Addition is effective in every successive reinvention of the situation. The quality of addition is, in the next place, brought to concretisation to division that has an applicability to assess the worth of the enrichment of the categories by comparing the scale of enrichment. The idea of comparison holds ground to the extent that the reality of transformation has meant to approach the reality to have synthesis by reducing the cruder form and enlisting the significant part of the situation. Ānandavardhana should like to make mention of the fact that the two categories, say, for example, *bhāva* and *vākya*, could be brought to be complete for the sake of ensuring an authoritative performance and the result that would be obtained would be assuredly the absolute form of the each. The continuity of division could be the necessary purpose for thoroughly laying down the conjunctions for the emergence of pure artistry. It would only be a matter of insisting upon the conjugal need of the necessary term for the universal in such a situation. At the end of the process of division, the range of idealisation substantially increases and to a great extent makes it convenient to interact and interpose all the variants of qualitative excellence together. It must be understood that this way of unifying the realisable proportion of language and experience is also the qualification for a greater commitment for a superior function of the art. In *dhvani*, the nature of art is exclusively something that could be seen and observed as a distinct displacement of one enriched variable towards other so much so that variation in the composite situation is kept in a state of motion. Consequently, the strength is further added to the wholesome situation. The question deserves to be asked as to how and why the functionality in art is proportional to the observance of absolute in the artistry. Mammaṭa and Abhinavagupta have examined the problem at length and affirmatively answered the question by suggesting the obvious transference of one enriched material into the other in the background of the height and expansion achieved by the artistic situation. Mammaṭa has to hold the ground that in each of such cases unity in intellection along with unity in the effect of intellection is retained. From this, it would be possible to find out a perfect groundwork for the same. Division among the categories or division by the categories is meaningful for the sake of adding concrete perspective to the qualitative situation. For that matter art is compounded by the framework of conceptualisation and the position of contents becomes appreciably enlarged. In *dhvani* system, the growth of medium and context to synchronise the artistry is eventually the result of structural addition and structural changes. To supplement this, the framework of multiplication is brought about. In this particular concern, the term "multiplication" comes to stand for an interpolation of inverse to the category, and therefore, it creates the considerable amount of variety and the extent of refinement. The multiplication of category with the category also introduces a condition of totality that necessarily presents a better form of the fine outcome of an artistic action. There can be an easy admittance of the fact that a refined content of the category impels similar form under the similar context in the similar category, hence, the adequacy of total situation is adjusted convincingly and forthrightly while multiplicative agents are intending expansion, assertive imposition of appropriate equivalent turns the perspective of artistry into the fulfilment of legitimate and rational occupation of comprehension. In other words, the probability of reliability on the act of comprehension is now basically a felt truth. We can understand from this that the cause and effect of advancing enrichment attend to the lateral conditionality of inquisition and for the same reason the acceptance of the instrument of transformation as a primary modifying unit is worth the interpretation. Ānandavardhana advocates the pertinence by speaking of वाच्यवाचकचारुत्वहेतूनां by the virtue of आलोकार्थी यथा

दीपशिखायां यत्नवाञ्जनाः. The culmination of formalistic approval of the structures is recognised till the time cognition is variously motivated. The form of interpolation that every inverse of accumulation approaches is precisely the factor that leads to the constitution of the absolute. The location of enriched variable within the category in the form of क्रमेण प्रतिभात्मानां would essentially invoke a graduation along रसाभावतदाभासतत्प्रशान्त्यादिरक्रमः. The actual strength of artistry, hence, is built and insisted through inter-modificational contents, which come as determined yet continuous replacement to these that are purposely not suited for the purpose. The other instruments of transformation like conjunction, injunction, inception, conception, similarly advance the centre of cognition lying right at the places of interaction where nearly all the contents are synchronised and adopted simultaneously to restore the adequacy of content to the context or medium to the content. In either of the cases, the principal concern would be to heighten the coordinates of conjunction so much so that the modification must yield an aggregate of ratiocination, concentration, absolute and totality. The condition of reversibility of the modifying contents is also one of the causes that strongly enter into the subsistence of super artistry, and accordingly, the ideals of *dhvani* maintain qua motif for the purpose of variously enriched artistic situation.

IV

The approval of synthesis and recognition of convergence as the basic constitution of universality and totality produce the effect that generates the various conditions of text textuality and texture of the categories. In *dhvani* and in the structuralist poetics, the adoption of the situation is maximum and full scale. *Dhvani* suggests a ratio-empirical model of textual authority and circumstance. For that matter, text is supposed to be the convergence of all the absolute and the total conjunctions, which have been active in the initiation of the process of evolution. It would mean that enrichment condition is activated with a precision and perfection and thus the result is obtained that foresees the event of completion. The applicability of such a method would complete the modification of *bhāva, vibhāva, anubhāva, sañcārībhāva, śabda, pada,* and *vākya* inasmuch as the strength of position and magnitude of direction are so sufficiently included into the curriculum of an ideal artistic production that every inventry of relation, interrelation, position, proposition, reason and cognition are brought together. There would also be the situation for which the commitment of presentation, exposition and association would find a score of worthy meaning. Thus the idealised *bhāva* would immediately state positivised and an equally functionally assorted universal for itself. This admits the regular transformation of content into context and content into the medium. Similarly, *śabda, pada, vākya, bhāva, vibhāva, anubhāva* and other categories obtain generative function whose extention is felt in the composite absolute. Textuality, on the other hand, is a manner of governing the condition of division and association that are brought within the artistic environment so much so that these attach themselves as the necessary movement to idealise the artistry of the concerned category. This states with certain precision for manifesting an event with necessary structural and functional proposition. This leads us to find out a worthy answer for the question as to what exactly is the text. The answer that Ānandavardhana and others would like to give would be squarely in relation to the creativity and the high function of artistry. For the matter of that, it must be insisted upon that in the material circumstances of creative situation encompasing refined categories along with the maturer forms of idealisation, the pursuit of text is accomplished. In the structuralist poetics, the rationality and empiricism of language and experience are compulsive and therefore the extent to which the evolution is obtained prepares the categories for the sake of comprehensibility and authenticity. Because of this, we can understand the emergence of two important possibilities — first, the skill of graduation along which the content and medium are hierarchised is randomly distributed, and, in the second place, the random distribution of the content attracts the consolidated signifiers. It is only for this reason that meaningful words are likely to invent a series of correlations with equally mature versions of the context of the given category. The role of signifiers in enhancing the suitablty and capability of synthesis and represent the foundation of resolution is also noteworthy and nearly in every signifier this dispensation is suitability fitted. On the further level of expansion, the continuation and synthesis are remarkable. The expression of exposition and interpretation of the realised models are confirmed. The actual necessity of looking at the nature of signification is finally resolved in the constitution of a composite conceptual frame from which assimilation and dissemination of value is prepared and obtained. It might be that the position of a signifier is either vertical or horizontal, yet, in either of the cases the modification of the content would be directly proportional to the scale of enrichment. In other words, the principle of modification admits the consistency of simultaneous retrieval and exposition of the heterogeneous contents within the categories. Thus the linear progression of the contents is received successfully in the cyclical manner of association. Between these two, the intention and necessity of resolving the refine models of language and experience, complete adequacy of context to the medium and medium to the content, is always examined and for this reason, change in the position and status of the letters, syllables, words, sentence, paragraph, thought, language and experience and the like could be essentially gathered up and mutated until every circumstance is a concrete universal in itself. In the structuralist poetics, linguistic attributes like words and letters and experiential models like experience and imagination are observed only with reference to a certain magnitude of concretisation they could obtain. For this reason, there is a committed reduction of the figurative contents within these categories and the phenomenon of reduction is expressive for the implicit association between two categories. In fact, it would be better to say that reduction is a determinant of positivisation and also at the same time a methodology of constituting a pure framework of rationality. In both the systems of creation, comprehension and valuation of an artistic situation, emphasis is laid on the fact that functional enrichment, precision and exclusion of a due proportion of figural inversion is imminent and in consequence the configuration of text is worked out.

V

The manifestation of resolution of an object into an event is brought about by suggesting the idealised varieties of experience and language, and, of which, metaphor has the concrete form of explicating and extending the ratiocination. In *dhvani* the role of metaphor is to add consequence to the formation. For this reason, it acts as an agent that brings about revival at the beginning of artistry and continuity towards the end of the whole situation by adopting and approaching synthesis of the content as the first principle. Ānandavardhana defines metaphor as a significant system of suggestion and would like therefore to assign a vast range of artistic functions to this figure of transformation. In the first place, it would actuate and confirm the presence of refined contents inasmuch as the event of inception takes off as the inference of the whole proposition, and because of this, the object that comes forth to rearrange and regroup the inferential content is certainly that which places each in a context of absolute precision. The development of form, that is so essential for the continuity of an artistic situation, is enhanced as an effect primarily, because of the fact that the contents enter into correlative set-up and the function of the structure of the categories is accordingly concentrated in the optimum locations. This therefore suggests the point that metaphorical activity could regroup and rearrange the possibility of transformation at any place and in any circumstance. Ānandavardhana's insistence proves to be of remarkable significance in that the progressing artistry adjusts the relative intensity on the basis of the hierarchy of the value. For this reason, appropriate meaning, exact meaning and truthful meaning could add to the expansion of the situation. Even otherwise, two enriched categories, say, for example, *bhāva* and *śabda* would induce a continuity of cyclical progression by virtue of advancing and retracting the positions of the absolute and the universals. Metaphor in that way is the finality, culmination of the growth of artistry, and, on that account, it yields a substance of complete artistic exposition. In the structuralist poetics, metaphor acts as a primordial formation wherein the immediacy of enrichment is purported to be aggravated. Saussure, Barthes, Jakobson, Genette, and Greimas have brought forth the contention that linear progression and cyclical displacement that ensure intersection of the categories at the point of culmination are most suitable for the creation of metaphor. For the same reason, every enriched formation entailing and gathering up of the content of language and experience are brought together, and accordingly, exposed to the continuous changes in terms of their structure and function. In consequence, one can easily understand how the preparatory model of metaphor intends a genuine and large-scale artistic effect. In *dhvani* and the structuralist poetics, synthesis, synchronisation, convergence and enrichment are the immediately realisable variants of the metaphor, and, on such an account, the creation of genuine artistry is accomplished.

VI

The common pursuit of transformation of an object into an event in both of the theories approaches a summation of exact cultural and religious standards and, for this reason, *dhvani* examines the necessity of building up an exceptional strength in the absolute that revolves around the presentation of indivisible and pure artistry. It follows from this that the higher level of enrichment of language and experience would mean universal assortment of cultural and religious categories, and accordingly, higher state of culture; supreme religious order would be founded upon the idealised linguistic and experiential models. Ānandavardhana's emphasis on "शृङ्गारश्य यांगिनो यात्नोदकुरूपानुबन्धनार्थे शर्वेष्ववेव प्रभेदेषु नानुप्रास प्रकाशक:" confirms the view that achievement of the absolute has to be having simultaneity of appearance in religio-social and socio-religious circumstances. Similarly, in the structuralist poetics, the explication of methodological frame of knowledge puts forth all the necessary objects of refinement and envisages the birth of an order of upgradation and expansion. Lévi Strauss and others, including Roland Barthes, have successfully implemented this and proved that continuity of linguistic system is also commensurate with similar changes of totality introduced into religious and cultural forms. Myth, as a consequence of socio-religious and socio-cultural displacement, is a worthy instrument of transformation. In fact, it acts as a modifier that has the business of presenting the completion of addition. To this extent, the structuralist poetics is very successful.

In both the tradition of inquisitive formations with regard to genuine artistic situation, emphasis is laid on the fact that there has to be a division within the artistry and each division must separate the contents so much so that the contents are idealised together. Having idealised these categories, these would obtain adequacy on their own and the event of meaning creation will be near at hand.

VII

Condition of formation and the configuration of presentation of the categories (*bhāva*, *vibhāva*, *anubhāva*, *sthāyībhāva*, *sañcārībhāva*, *ālambana* and *uddīpana*; word, letter, syllable, paragraph, thought, imagination, language, experience) uphold the basic necessity of initiating and accomplishing the modification of an object into an event and hence an ideal artistry is specifically designated. In *dhvani*, the manner of creation and exposition is based on the agents and agencies of change and for this reason addition, multiplication, subtraction, injunction, conjunction, conception and inception would act as the instruments which not only restore the adequacy but also bring about the fixation of content as content and form as form, and thus, correspondence is harmonised. In the structuralist manner of comprehension, constitution and valuation of language and experience as two explicit models of enrichment stand to the truth that these categories are precisely oriented towards changes in structure and function at every stage of growth and expansion, consequently, the highest intensity of artistry is observable once the process of evolution is complete. In both *dhvani* and the structuralist poetics strength, commitment, conviction, progress, expansion and universalisation of artistry are confirmed and assured at the behest of participating medium, content, context and the categories of artistic creation, and that is precisely the truth and reality that has been so well realised and understood.

Bibliography

Part A : Dhvani

Abhayankar, K.V., *A Dictionary of Sanskrit Grammar*, Baroda: Oriental Institute, 1977.

Abhinavagupta, *Abhinavabhāratī*, Madras: n.p., n.d.

Abhinavagupta, *Abhinavabhārtī*, ed. and tr. Acharya Vishveshwar, Delhi: Oxford University Press, 1960.

———, *Locana with Prakāśa*, tr. Acarya Jagannath Pathak, Varanasi: Chowkhamba Vidya Bhavan, 1965.

Amarukakavi, *Amaruśataka*, Bombay: Kāvyāmalā 18, 1916. Print.

Ānandavardhana, *Dhvanyāloka*, ed. & tr. K. Krishnamoorthy, Varanasi: Motilal Banarsidass, 1974.

Arthur, A. Macdonell, *Sanskrit-English Dictionary*, London: Longmans Green and Co. and New York, 1893.

Awasthi, Brahamamitra, *Alaṅkāra-Kośa*. Delhi: Indu Prakashan, 1983.

Bāṇabhaṭṭa, *Harṣacarita*, Bombay: n.p., 1980.

Beck, Guy. L., *Sonic Theology: Hinduism and Sacred Sound*, Delhi: Motilal Banarsidass, 1995.

Bhāmaha, *Kāvyālaṁkāra*, ed. Pratap Rudra Yasobhusana, tr. P.V. Naganath Sastry, Tanjore: n.p., 1927.

Bharatamuni, *Nāṭyā-Śāstra*, ed. Kāvyamāla & Kashi Sanskrit Series, Banaras: Chowkhamba Sanskrit Series Office, 1929.

Bharatamuni, *Nāṭya-Śāstra*, ed. Sahityacarya Madhusudan Shastri. Banaras: Chowkhamba Sanskrit Series Office, 1929.

Bhartṛhari, *Śatakatrayam*, ed. Krishnamani Tripathi, Varanasi: Chowkhamba Vidya Bhavan, 2002.

———, *Vākyapadīyam*, Varanasi: Sampurnanand Sanskrit Vishwavidyalaya, 1980.

Bhāsa, *Swapnavasavadattam*, Varanasi: Chowkhamba Surbharti Prakashan, 1976.

Bhatt, V.P., *Vyutpattivāda*, Delhi: Eastern Book Linkers, 1990.

Bhaṭṭojidīkṣita, *Siddhāntakaumudī*, Bombay: n.p., 1929.

Bhavabhūti, *Uttararāmacarita*, ed. P.V. Kane, Bombay: n.p., 1928.

Bhoja, *Sarasvatīkanthābharaṇa*, ed. Kāvyāmalā 95. Bombay: n.p., 1925.

Chatterji, K.N., *Word and Its Meaning: A New Perspective*, Varanasi: Chowkhamba Orientation, 1980.

Daṇḍin, *Kāvyādarśa*, ed. Premchandra Tarkavagisha, Calcutta: n.p., Śaka 1803.

Dange, Sindhu S., *Aspects of Speech in Vedic Ritual*, New Delhi: Aryan Books International, 1996.

De, S.K., *Studies in the History of Sanskrit Poetics*, London: n.p., 1923 & 1925.

Dhanañjaya, *Daśarūpakam*, ed. Bhola Shankar Vyas, Varanasi: Chowkhamba Sanskrit Series, 1955.

Gosvami, Sri Rupa, *Bhakti-Rasāmṛta Sindhuḥ*, tr. Pridandi Swami, Vrindaban: Institute of Oriental Philosophy, 1965.

Hemchandra, *Kāvyānuśāsana*, ed. R.C. Parikh and V.M. Kulkarni, Bombay: Sri Mahavira Jaina Vidyalaya, 1964.

Hiriyanna, M., *Indian Aesthetics*, Poona: Bori, 1922.

Jagannatha, Panditraj, *Rasagaṅgādhara*, ed. Madhusudan Shastri with Marmaprakash of Nagesh Bhatta, Varanasi: B.H.U. Press, 17th Century AD

Jagannatha, *Rasagaṅgādhara*, Kāvyamālā 12. Bombay: n.p., 1916.

Jayadeva, *Prasannarāghava*, ed. W.L.S. Pansikar, Bombay: NSP, 1922.

Jha, Kalanatha, *Figurative Poetry in Sanskrit Literature*, Delhi: Motilal Banarsidass, 1975.

Jha, Mahāmahopādhyāya Sir Ganganatha, *Kāvyaprakāśa of Mammaṭa with English Translation* (revised), Varanasi: Bharatiya Vidya Prakashan, 1996.

Jhalakikar, *Nyāyakośa*, Poona: Bombay Sanskrit and Prakrit Series No. XLIX, 1928.

Kālidāsa, *Abhijñānaśākuntalam*, ed. A.B. Gajendragadkar, Surat: The Popular Publishing House, 1962.

Kālidāsa, *Abhijñānaśākuntalam*, Delhi: Motilal Banarsidass, 1969.

Kālidāsa, *Abhijñānaśākuntalam*, ed. Subodha Chandra Pant, Delhi: n.p., 1983.

———, *Raghuvaṁśa*, ed. Sankar P. Pandit, Bombay: Nirnaya Sagar Press, 1872.

Kane, P.V., *History of Alaṁkāra Literature in his Edition to the Sāhityadarpaṇa*, Bombay: n.p., 1923.

Kauṇḍabhaṭṭa, *The Samāsaśaktinirṇaya*, ed. Banamali Biswal, Allahabad: Padmaja Prakashan, 1995.

Kṣemendra, *Aucitya-Vicāra-Carcā*, ed. Kāvyamālā Part I, Bombay: n.p., 1889.

Kuntaka, *Vakrokti-Jīvita*, ed. S.K. De. Calcutta: n.p., 1928.

Māgha, *Śiśupāla-Vadha*, ed. Jivananda Vidyasagara, Calcutta: n.p., 1889.

Mahimabhaṭṭa, *Vyaktiviveka with Vyaktivivekavyākhyā*, Trivendrum: T.S.S., 1909.

Mammaṭa, *Kāvyaprakāśa*, ed. Dr. Sir Ganganatha Jha, Delhi: Bhartiya Vidya Prakashan, 1965.

Mammaṭa, *Kāvyaprakāśa*, ed. Vāmanācārya Jhalkikar, Bombay: Bombay Sanskrit and Prakrit Series, 1921.

Nobel, J., *Foundations of Indian Poetry*, Calcutta: n.p., 1925.

Panday, K.C., *Comparative Aesthetics*, 2 vols., *Western Aesthetics*, Varanasi: Chowkhamba Sanskrit Series, 1972.

———, *Comparative Aesthetics*, 2 vols. *Indian Aesthetics*, Varanasi: Chowkhamba Sanskrit Series, n.d.

Panditraj, Jagannatha, *Rasagaṅgādhara*, ed. Madhusudan Shastri with Marmaprakash of Nagesh Bhatta, Varanasi: B.H.U. Press, n.d.

Pāṇini, *Aṣṭādhyāyī*, ed. & trans. S.C. Vasu, Delhi: Motilal Banarsidass, 1962.

Rājaśekhara, *Kāvyamīmāṁsā*, ed. Gaekwad Oriental Series No. 1 Baroda: n.p., 1924.

Rudraṭa, *Kāvyalaṅkāra with the Commentary of Namisdhan*, Bombay: Kāvyamālā 2, 1928.

Ruyyaka, *Alaṅkāra-Sarvasva with the Commentary of Samudrabandha*, Trivendram: T.S.S, 1926.

Sankaran, A., *Some Aspects of Literary Criticism*, Madras: University of Madras, 1929.

Sankrityayan, Rahul, *Sanskrit Kāvyadhārā*, Allahabad: Kitab Mahal Sammelan Mudralaya, 1957.

Shastri, Gaurinath, *The Philosophy of Word and Meaning*, Calcutta: Calcutta Sanskrit College Research Series No. 2, 1959.

Tiwari, R.S., *A Critical Approach to Classical Indian Poetics*, Delhi, Varanasi: Chowkhamba Sanskrit Series, 1984.

Urubshurow, Victoria, *Indian Mantra as Transformative Speech Act*, Aligarh: Aligarh Oriental Series. No. 2, 1985.

Vāgbhaṭa, *Kāvyānuśāsana*, Bombay: Kāvyamālā 43, 1915.

Vallabhadeva, *Sabhāṣitavatī*, ed. Peterson, Bombay: n.p., 1886.

Vāmana, *Kāvyālaṁkāra-Sūtra-Vṛtti*, Śrīraṅgam: Sri Vānivilāsa Sastra Series 5, 1909.

Veda Vyāsa, *Mahābhārata*, tr. Ramnarayan Datta Shastri, n.p., 1955.

Viśvanātha, *Sāhityadarpaṇa*, ed. Maheshwar Bhatt, Bombey: Motilal Banarsidass, 1938.

Part B : Structuralism

Barthes, Roland, *Action Sequence: Patterns of Literary Style*, ed. J. Strelka, Pennsylvania: State University Press, 1971.

———, "Critical Essays", in *Structuralism and since*: From Levi – Strauss to Derrida, ed. John Sturrock, New York: OUP, 1960.

———, *Critique et Verite*, Paris: 1966.

———, *Mythologies*, Seuil, Paris, 1970.

———, *Sade, Fourier and Loyola*, Paris: Sevil, 1971.

———, "To write: An Intransitive Verb", in *The Languages of Criticism and the Science of Man*, ed. R. Mackey and E. Donato. Baltimore: Johns Hopkins Press, 1970.

Baudelaire, Charles, *Les Fleurs du mal: The Complete Text of the Flowers of Evil in a New Translation*, trans. Richard Howard, Boston: n.p., 1982.

Bierwisch, Manfred, Poetics and Linguistics, in *Linguistics and Literary Style*, ed. D. Freeman, New York: Holt Rinehart, 1970.

Bloch, B. (with G.L. Trager), *Outline of Linguistic Analysis*, Baltimore: Waverly, 1942.

———, *Generative Grammar and the Theory of Literature*, 3 vols Bucharest: Rumanian Academy, 1969.

Boon, James A., *From Symbolism to Structuralism*: Lévi Strauss in a Literary Tradition, Oxford: Blackwell, 1972.

Booth, Stephen, *On the Value of Hamlet, Reinterpretation of Elizabethan Drama* (English Institute Essays), ed. Robkin Columbia, New York: n.p., 1969.

Booth, Wayne, *The Rhetoric of Fiction*, Chicago: University of Chicago Press, 1961.

Brooks-Rose, Christine, *A Grammar of Metaphor*, London: Secker & Warburg, 1958.

Brooks, Cleanth, *The Well-Wrought Urn*, New York: Harcourt & Brace, 1947.

Burns, Eligabeth and Tom, eds., *Sociology of Literature and Drama*, Harmondsworth: Penguin, 1973.

Chatmon, Seymour, ed., *Essays on the Language of Literature*, Boston: Houghton Miffin, 1967.

———, ed. *Literary Style: A Symposium*, New York: Oxford University Press, 1971.

Chomsky, Noam, *Aspects of the Theory of Syntax*, Cambridge & Mass: MIT, 1965.

———, *Current Issues in Linguistic Theory*, The Hague: Mouton, 1964.

———, *Language and Mind*, New York: Harcourt Brace, 1968.

———, *Syntactic Structure*, The Hague: Mouton, 1957.

Corvez, Maurice, *Les Structuralistes*, Paris: Aubier-Montaigne, Toronto: UTP, 1953.

Culler, Jonathan, *The Pursuit of Signs*, New York: Routledge, 1981.

Culler, Jonathan, *Structuralist Poetics*, London: Routledge, 1989.

———, "The Linguistic Basis of Structuralism", in *Structuralism: An Introduction*, ed. D. Robey, n.p.: Oxford University Press, 1973.

Dante, *Divine Comedy*: Inferno. ed. & trans. Israel Golcang in Temple Classics, Harward: HUP, 1946.

De George, Richard and Fernande, eds., *The Structuralists*, New York: Doubleday, 1972.

Dijk, Ten A. Van, *Some Aspects of Grammars*, The Hague: Mouton, 1972.

Donne, John, *The Complete Poetry and Selected Prose*, ed. John Hayward, New York : The Modern Library, 1946.

Eichenbaum, Boris, "The Theory of the 'Formal Method'", in *Russian Formalist Criticism*, ed. L.T. Lemon and M.J. Reis. Lincoln: University of Nebraska Press, 1965.

Empson, William, *Seven Types of Ambiguity*, Harmondsworth: Penguin, 1961.

Forrest–Thomson, Veronica, *Poetic Artifice: A Theory of Twentieth Century Poetry*, Oxford: Blackwell, 1974.

Freeman, Donald, ed., *Linguistics and Literary Style*, New York: Holt Rinehart, 1970.

Frye, Northrop, *Anatomy of Criticism*. New York: Atheneum, 1965.

Garvin, Paul, *On Linguistic Method*, The Hague: Mouton, 1964.

Genette, Gérard, *Figures*, Paris: Seuil, 1966.

Goodman, Nelson, *The Language of Art*, London: Oxford University Press, 1969.

Greimas, A.J., ed., *Sign, Language, Culture*. The Hague: Mouton, 1970.

Guillen, Claudio, *Literature as System*, Princeton: Princeton University Press, 1971.

Halliday, M.A.K., "Descriptive Linguistics" in *Literary Studies: In Patterns of Language'*, London: Longmans, 1966.

———, "Language Structure and Language Function", in *New Horizons in Lingusitics*, ed. J. Lyons, Harmondsworth: Penguin, 1970.

———, "Linguistic Function and Literary Style", *in Literary Style: A Symposium*, ed. S. Chatman, New York: Oxford University Press, 1971.

Harris, Zellig, *Methods of Structural Linguistics*, Chicago: University of Chicago Press, 1951.

Hartman, Geoffrey, *Beyond Formalism*, New Haven: Yale University Press, 1970.

Heath, Stephen, *Towards Textual Semiotics: Signs of the Times*, Cambridge: Granta, 1971.

Hockett, C.A., A *Course in Modern Linguistics*, New York: Macmillan, 1958.

———, *A Manual of Phonology*, Bloomington: Indiana University Press, 1955.

———, *The State of the Art*, The Hague: Mouton, 1967.

Homer, *Iliad*. trans. George Chapman, Hertfordshire: Wordsworth Classics, 2003.

Householder, Fred, *Linguistic Speculations*, n.p.: Cambridge University Press, 1971. Print.

Jakobson, Roman, "Linguistics and Poetics", in *Style in Language*, ed. T. Sebeok, Cambridge: MIT Press, 1960.

Jakobson, Roman, *Modern Criticism and Theory*, ed. David Lodge. London & New York: Longman, 1991.

Jainson, Fredric, *Marxism and Form*, n.p.: Princeton University Press, 1971.

Kenner, Hugh, "Some Post-Symbolist Structures", in *Literary Theory and Structure*, ed. F. Brady et al., New Haven: Yale University Press, 1973.

Koch, Walter, *Recurrence and A Three Modal Approach to Poetry*, The Hague: Mouton, 1966.

Lane, Michael, ed., *Structuralism: A Reader*, London: Cape, 1970.

Leach, Edmund, *Genesis as Myth and Other Essays*, London: Cape, 1969.

———, "Language and Anthropology", in *Linguistic at Large*, ed. Minnis, London: Gouancz, 1971.

———, *Lévi Strauss*, London: Fontana, 1970.

———, ed., *The Structural Study of Myth and Totemism*, London: Tavistock, 1967.

Leech, G.N., *A Linguistic Guide to English Poetry*, London: Longmans, 1969.

Lengacre, Robert, *Grammar Discovery Procedures*, The Hague: Mouton, 1964. Print.

Lepschy, G.C., *A Survey of Structural Linguistics*, London: Faber & Faber, 1970.

Levi, Jiri, "Generative Poetics", in *Sign, Language, Culture*, ed. A.J. Greimas, The Hague: Mouton, 1970.

Levin, Samuel, "The Conventions of Poetry", in *Literary Style: A Symposium*, ed. S. Chatman. New York: Oxford University Press, 1971.

———, *Linguistic Structures in Poetry*, The Hague: Mouton, 1962.

Lévi Strauss, Claude, *Structural Anthropology*, tr. Claire and Brooke, London: Basic Books, INC., 1963.

Lyons, John, *Introduction to Theoretical Linguistics*, n.p.: Cambridge University Press, 1968.

———, ed., *New Horizons in Linguistics*, Harmondsworth: Penguin, 1970.

———, *Structural Semantics*, Oxford: Blackwell, 1963.

Macksey, Richard, ed., *The Language of Criticism and the Science of Man*, Baltimore: Johns Hopkins Press, 1970.

Man, Paulde, *Blindness and Insight: Essays in the Rhetoric of Contemporary Criticism*, New York: Oxford University Press, 1971.

Marvell, Andrew, *To his Coy Mistress in Metaphysical Poets*, ed. Helen Gardner, London: OUP, 1972.

Mukarovsky, J., "The Esthetics of Language", in *A Prague School Reader*, ed. P. Garvin, Washington: Georgetown University Press, 1964.

———, "Standard Language and Poetic Language", in *A Prague School Reader*, ed. Garvin, Washington: Georgetown University Press, 1964.

Patañjali, *Mahābhaṣya*, N.p.: n.p. 1876.

Pike, Kenneth, *Language in Relation to a Unified Theory of Human Behaviour*, The Hague: Mouton, 1967.

Price, Martin, "The Fictional Contract", in *Literary Theory and Structure*, ed. F. Brady et al. New Haven: Yale University Press, 1973.

Robey, David (ed.), *Structuralism: An Introduction*, London: Oxford University Press, 1973.

Saumjan, S.K., "Semiotics and the Theory of Generative Grammar", in *Sign, Language, Culture*, ed. A.J. Greimas, The Hague: Mouton, 1970.

Saussure, Ferdinand De, *Course in General Linguistics* ed. Bally and Albert Sechchage, tr. Wade Basking from the French, London: Peter Owen, 1960.

Searle, John, *Speech Acts*, n.p.: Cambridge University Press, 1969.

Shakespeare, William, *The Illustrated Stratford Shakespeare*, Exter Books, New York: n.p., 1984.

Ullmann, Stephen, *Language and Style*, Oxford: Blackwell, 1964.

———, *Principles of Semantics*, Oxford: Blackwell, 1963.

Wellek, Rene, *Theory of Literature*, 3rd edn., London: Cape, 1966.

Willen, Anthony, *The Language of the Self*, Baltimore: Johns Hopkins Press, 1968.

———, *System and Structure: Essays on Communication and Exchange*, London: Tavistock, 1972.

Index